simplylitefood

simplylitefood

The Australian Women's
Weekly
cookbooks

contents

starters and snacks

prawn cakes with choy sum

per serving 11.1g fat; 671kJ

1.25kg	uncooked prawns, peeled, deveined
3 tsps	finely grated fresh ginger
2	birdseye chillies, seeded, chopped
1 tsp	finely grated lemon rind
1 tsp	finely grated lime rind
2 tbsps	olive oil
500g	choy sum, trimmed
80ml	(⅓ cup) sweet chilli sauce
2 tbsps	soy sauce

Blend or process prawns, ginger, chillies and rinds until well combined. Divide mixture into 8, shape into patties. Heat oil in large pan, cook patties in batches until golden brown and just cooked through; keep warm. Boil, steam or microwave choy sum until just wilted, drain well. Serve prawn cakes and choy sum with combined sweet chilli and soy sauce.

serves 4

Distinguishable by its small, yellow flowers and its mild mustard taste, choy sum (or Chinese flowering cabbage) has fleshy white stems and tender green leaves. It's best stir-fried, steamed or in soups.

*"One cannot think well,
love well, sleep well,
if one has not dined well."*

VIRGINIA WOOLF

smoked salmon with dill pancakes

per serving 1.9g fat; 1029kJ

150g	**(1 cup) self-raising flour**
	Salt and pepper
160ml	**(2/3 cup) skim milk**
2	**egg whites**
1 tbsp	**chopped fresh dill**
100g	**sliced smoked salmon**
200ml	**low-fat plain yogurt**
1 tbsp	**seeded mustard**
50g	**(1 cup) snow pea sprouts**
2 tbsps	**baby capers**
12	**baby gherkins**

Sift flour, salt and pepper into a bowl. Make a well in the centre, add milk and egg whites, whisk until smooth; stir in dill. Heat a non-stick frying pan to medium-low, spray with cooking oil spray. Drop 60ml (1/4 cup) of mixture into pan, spread quickly into a circle about 10cm in diameter. Cook for 20 seconds or until bubbles begin to appear on the surface. Turn over, cook until browned. Remove from pan, repeat with remaining mixture. Serve pancakes topped with smoked salmon, combined yogurt and mustard, snow pea sprouts, capers and gherkins.

serves 4

Ciabatta is the Italian word for an old slipper or shoe; this crusty, slightly sour-tasting bread is so called because its baggy, roughly oval shape resembles a trusty old slipper.

roasted tomatoes and field mushrooms on
garlic bruschetta

per serving 9.9g fat; 941kJ

4	**large (360g) egg tomatoes, halved**
8	**large field mushrooms, thickly sliced**
1 tbsp	**fresh oregano leaves**
4	**thick slices ciabatta bread**
1	**clove garlic, peeled**
2 tbsps	**olive oil**
12	**baby spinach leaves**

Place tomatoes, cut side up, and mushrooms in large, oiled, ovenproof baking dish, sprinkle with oregano. Roast in moderately hot oven (200°C) for 15 minutes or until lightly browned and soft.

Toast ciabatta under grill, rub with garlic clove, brush with oil, and top with tomatoes and mushroom mixture. Garnish with spinach leaves before serving.

serves 4

crispy spring rolls

per serving 12.6g fat; 792kJ

¼   barbecued chicken (ie, 125g meat)

2   green onions

1   large (180g) carrot, coarsely grated

⅓ cup   fresh coriander leaves

2 tsps   grated fresh ginger

¼ tsp   sesame oil

½ tsp   Chinese five-spice

12   22cm-round rice paper sheets

2 tbsps   peanut oil

Sweet chilli sauce, for dipping

Remove skin and bones from chicken, shred the meat. Cut green onions into thin strips about 6cm long. Combine chicken, green onions, carrot, coriander, ginger, sesame oil and five-spice. Lay rice paper sheets out on work surface, brush both sides with water, stand 3 minutes or until softened. Divide chicken mixture between rice paper, fold in the sides, roll tightly.

Heat half the peanut oil in a non-stick frying pan, add half the rolls, cook over medium heat for 3 minutes or until crisp, lightly browned and warmed through; toss pan occasionally to give even browning. Repeat with remaining peanut oil and rolls. Serve with chilli sauce.

serves 4 (makes 12)

mini garlic
potato omelettes

per omelette 5.1g fat; 442kJ

3	medium (600g) potatoes
1 tbsp	olive oil
3	cloves garlic, crushed
4	eggs
	Salt and pepper, to taste
	Snow pea sprouts for garnish, optional

Wash the potatoes and cut, unpeeled, into wafer-thin slices, using a mandolin slicer or the slicing side of a grater. Pat the potatoes dry with absorbent paper.

Heat oil in a non-stick frying pan, cook potatoes and garlic over medium heat for 4 minutes or until softened and browned, turning often; drain on absorbent paper.

Whisk eggs with salt and pepper.

Preheat oven to moderate (180°C). Lay 8 x 7cm oiled tart tins on a baking tray. Divide potatoes between tins, pour over egg mixture. Bake omelettes for 15 minutes or until just set. Loosen the omelettes in the tins. Serve hot or cold, in or out of the tins.

makes 8

"There is no such thing as a little garlic."

ARTHUR BAER

oyster shooters
with lime and tabasco

per serving 0.4g fat; 64kJ

1	lime
16	large rock oysters
2 tbsps	Tabasco sauce, approx
	Freshly ground pepper

Cut lime into thin wedges.

Divide oysters between 8 small shot glasses. Drizzle with Tabasco to taste, sprinkle with pepper, and top with lime. Serve immediately.

serves 8

"You never get a second chance to make a first impression."

WILL ROGERS

spiced meatballs
with peach chutney

per meatball 0.9g fat; 185kJ

250g	pork and veal mince
125g	leg ham off the bone, finely chopped
35g	(1/3 cup) packaged breadcrumbs
4	cloves garlic, crushed
1/2 tsp	ground coriander
1/2 tsp	ground cumin
1/4 tsp	ground cayenne pepper
1/4 tsp	ground nutmeg
1/4 cup	chopped fresh parsley
125ml	(1/2 cup) peach chutney

Preheat oven to moderately hot (200°C). Combine all ingredients, except the chutney, in a bowl, mix well. Divide mixture into 16 meatballs, place on a baking tray. Bake for 15 minutes or until lightly browned. Skewer each meatball with a toothpick, serve hot or cold, with peach chutney for dipping.

makes 16

*This recipe is a delicious example of tapa – those tasty appetisers from Spain.
In Spanish bars and restaurants, tapas are served free with a drink; the reasoning
is that the food will keep patrons sober and keep them going back for more.*

The best rice to use for sushi is koshihikari, a premium short-grain variety not to be confused with sticky or glutinous rice, which is used mainly for desserts.

tuna sushi rolls

per roll 1g fat; 1256kJ

800g	(4 cups) sushi rice
125ml	(½ cup) rice vinegar
75g	(⅓ cup) sugar
½ tsp	salt
12	sheets toasted nori
240g	yellowfin sashimi tuna, thinly sliced
2	(260g) Lebanese cucumbers, seeded, thinly sliced
90g	(⅓ cup) pickled ginger
1 tsp	wasabi paste
12	garlic chives

Add rice to large pan of boiling water; boil, uncovered, until just tender. Drain, stand rice 5 minutes; stir in combined vinegar, sugar and salt. Cool. Place one sheet of nori, rough side up, on damp bamboo sushi mat. Dip fingers in water and spread a twelfth of the rice mixture over nori, leaving a 4cm strip on short side furthest away from you; press rice firmly in place. Using fingers, make a lengthways hollow across centre of rice. Place a twelfth of each of tuna, cucumber, ginger, wasabi and chives in hollow. Starting at edge closest to you, use mat to roll the tuna nori, pressing firmly as you roll. Secure with 4cm strip at end. Repeat with remaining ingredients.

makes 12 rolls

artichoke dip

per tbsp 1.6g fat; 113kJ

400g	**can artichokes in water**
60g	**(¼ cup) low-fat mayonnaise**
	Freshly ground black pepper
2 tbsps	**low-fat ricotta cheese**
40g	**(⅓ cup) low-fat grated cheddar cheese**
¼ tsp	**ground paprika**
2	**medium (240g) carrots**

Drain artichokes, chop roughly. Combine in a food processor with mayonnaise, pepper, ricotta and cheddar cheese. Beat until just combined. Serve sprinkled with paprika. Cut carrots into long, thin slices, serve with dip.

makes 1⅓ cups (16 tbsps)

"The smell and taste of things remain poised a long time, like souls, ready to remind us."
MARCEL PROUST

Guest Chef
Peter Doyle
Cicada

roasted beetroot and orange salad with orange oil

per serving 14.8g fat; 1110kJ

2	large (400g) beetroot
2 tbsps	pine nuts
24	(500g) asparagus spears
2 tsps	olive oil
2 tsps	walnut oil*
1 tbsp	white wine vinegar
1	(225g) curly endive, leaves separated
2	bulbs red witlof, leaves separated
2	blood oranges, peeled, sliced**

orange oil

125ml	(½ cup) strained blood orange juice**
1 tbsp	lemon juice
1 tbsp	grapeseed oil*

Preheat oven to moderate (180°C). Trim leaves from beetroot, wrap unpeeled beetroot in foil. Bake for 1 hour or until tender; cool. Peel beetroot, cut each into 12 wedges. Spread pine nuts on a tray, bake for 10 minutes or until brown. Add asparagus to a large saucepan of boiling water, cook for 1 minute, drain, rinse under cold water.

Combine olive oil, walnut oil and vinegar in a bowl, add endive and witlof, toss until combined.

To serve, arrange leaves on serving plates, top with beetroot, pine nuts, asparagus, and oranges. Drizzle with orange oil.

Orange oil: Combine orange and lemon juice in a small saucepan, cook over medium heat for 5 minutes or until reduced and syrupy; cool. Stir in oil.

* Walnut and grapeseed oils can be purchased from most delicatessens. If unavailable, use olive oil.
** Blood oranges are available in winter. At other times, use navels instead.

serves 4

vietnamese-style salmon and rice paper rolls

per roll 3.5g fat; 540kJ

1/2	small (35g) carrot
1/2	small stick celery
1/4	small (50g) leek
25g	(1/3 cup) bean sprouts
1/2	small (50g) Spanish onion, finely sliced
8	16cm-round sheets dried rice paper
8	small slices smoked salmon
60ml	(1/4 cup) sweet soy sauce
2	birdseye chillies, finely chopped

thai dressing

1	birdseye chilli, chopped
2 tsps	grated fresh ginger
1	clove garlic, crushed
1 tbsp	finely chopped lemon grass
1 tbsp	chopped fresh coriander leaves
1 tbsp	chopped fresh mint leaves
1 tsp	fish sauce
1 tbsp	light coconut milk
2 tbsps	lime juice
2 tbsps	water

Cut carrot, celery and leek into fine straws about 8cm long. Combine with bean sprouts, onion and 2 tbsps of the Thai dressing. Soak rice paper sheets in cold water for 1 minute or until they feel pliable, drain. Lay salmon slices on each sheet. Lay vegetables along one side of each sheet. Roll tightly to enclose the vegetables, tucking in the ends as you roll. Serve with 2 dipping sauces: remaining Thai dressing and combined soy sauce and chillies.

Thai dressing: Combine all ingredients in a blender, blend until smooth.

makes 8 rolls

red beef and lemon pizza

per serving 8.7g fat; 1203kJ

350g	beef fillet
2 tbsps	red curry paste
1	medium (170g) Spanish onion, finely sliced
1 tbsp	finely grated lemon rind
1	long loaf pide
2 tbsps	tomato paste
2 tbsps	chicken stock
90g	(3/4 cup) grated reduced-fat cheddar cheese
30g	lamb's lettuce, washed

Remove fat from beef. Combine beef and red curry paste in small bowl. Cook beef in heated, non-stick pan until well browned all over and cooked as desired (about 5 minutes for medium-rare); slice. Keep warm.

Cook onion and rind in same pan for about 3 minutes or until onion is soft. Spread pide with combined tomato paste and stock. Top with cheese and onion mixture. Bake in very hot oven (230°C) for 10 minutes or until cheese melts. Top with beef and lamb's lettuce.

serves 6

pork and veal kofta

per serving 4g fat; 928kJ

500g	pork and veal mince
2 tsps	ground cumin
2	cloves garlic, crushed
1	small (80g) onion, chopped finely
2 tbsps	finely chopped dried apricots
2 tbsps	chopped fresh coriander leaves
1 tsp	hot paprika
90g	fresh chow mein noodles (or extremely thin fresh egg noodles), chopped

yogurt sauce

180ml	(3/4 cup) low-fat plain yogurt
1 tbsp	chopped fresh mint leaves
1 tsp	ground cumin
1 tsp	sugar

Combine mince, cumin, garlic, onion, apricots, coriander, paprika and noodles in a large bowl. Roll level tablespoons of mixture into oval-shaped kofta; thread 3 kofta onto each skewer.

Cook kofta, in batches, in heated oiled grill pan (or grill or barbecue), until browned and cooked through. Serve kofta with yogurt sauce.

Yogurt sauce: Combine all ingredients in small bowl.

serves 4

vietnamese-style salmon and rice paper rolls

red beef and lemon pizza

pork and veal kofta

soups

fresh vegetable consomme

per serving 2.8g fat; 245kJ

1 tbsp	whole black peppercorns
4	cloves garlic
2	bay leaves
2	sticks celery
2	medium (240g) carrots
15g	butter
1	medium (350g) leek, sliced
1.5 litres	(6 cups) water
1	large vegetable stock cube, crumbled
200g	broccoli, chopped

Tie peppercorns, garlic and bay leaves in muslin. Cut celery and carrots into short strips. Heat butter in large saucepan, cook leek over low heat for about 5 minutes or until leek is soft. Add the water, stock cube and muslin bag, bring to boil, reduce heat, add vegetables, simmer for about 5 minutes or until vegetables are just tender. Discard muslin bag.

NB: Consomme can be made a day ahead. Cover; refrigerate overnight.

serves 6

red cabbage and apple soup

per serving 0.9g fat; 460kJ

1	**medium (350g) leek, chopped**
1	**clove garlic, crushed**
240g	**(3 cups) shredded red cabbage**
125ml	**(½ cup) tomato juice**
2 tsps	**balsamic vinegar**
1	**large (200g) green apple, peeled, cored, chopped**
1	**large (300g) potato, peeled, chopped**
1 litre	**(4 cups) chicken stock**
2 tsps	**fresh lemon thyme leaves**

Cook leek and garlic in large, heated, non-stick saucepan, stirring until leek is tender. Add cabbage, juice, vinegar, apple, potato, stock and leaves. Simmer, covered, 25 minutes or until potato is tender. Blend or process soup in batches until smooth. Reheat without boiling. Divide soup between serving bowls, top with extra lemon thyme leaves if desired.

serves 4

Lemon thyme, like other herbs, is best purchased the day before, or the actual day, you intend using it. To keep any unused lemon thyme fresh, wrap it, unwashed, in paper towelling and store in a sealed plastic container in the refrigerator.

green pea and chestnut soup

per serving 2.8g fat; 742kJ

2 tsps	**olive oil**
1	**medium (150g) brown onion, coarsely chopped**
1	**clove garlic, crushed**
1.5 litres	**(6 cups) chicken or vegetable stock**
1kg	**frozen green peas**
70g	**(¼ cup) chestnut puree**

Heat oil in large pan; cook onion and garlic until onion is soft. Stir in stock and peas; bring to boil, simmer, uncovered, about 10 minutes or until peas are tender. Blend or process pea mixture, in batches, until smooth. Just before serving, return soup to pan with puree, stir over low heat until soup is hot. Serve with wholegrain bread or low-fat crackers, if desired.

serves 6

minestrone

per serving 3.4g fat; 1392kJ

2 tsps	olive oil
2	large (360g) carrots, coarsely chopped
1	medium (350g) leek, thickly sliced
2	large (300g) zucchini, coarsely chopped
3 litres	(12 cups) water or vegetable stock
2 tbsps	tomato paste
4	large (1kg) ripe tomatoes, coarsely chopped
135g	(3/4 cup) small macaroni pasta
165g	(3/4 cup) risoni pasta
200g	green beans, trimmed
2	thick slices fruit bread

Heat oil in large pan, cook carrots, leek and zucchini, stirring, until leek is soft. Stir in the water, paste and tomatoes; simmer, uncovered, 10 minutes or until vegetables are tender.

Stir in pasta and beans, bring to boil, simmer 10 minutes or until pasta is tender.

Meanwhile, to make croutons, cut bread into 2cm cubes. Place bread in lightly oiled baking dish, bake in moderate oven (180°C) about 10 minutes or until bread is golden brown. Stir occasionally. Serve minestrone with croutons.

serves 6

Choose a leek with a clean, white base and fresh-looking, dark-green top. Smaller leeks are the more tender and have a delicate, mild, onion flavour.

seafood gow gees
with fresh pea stock

per serving 6.4g fat; 1857kJ

350g	uncooked king prawns
125g	salmon fillet
2	green onions
1	small red chilli
1 tbsp	chopped fresh coriander
1/8 tsp	sesame oil
32	gow gee wrappers
625ml	(2 1/2 cups) well-flavoured fish stock
250g	(1 2/3 cups) shelled fresh peas (ie, approx 670g unshelled)
1 tsp	light soy sauce
1	clove garlic, halved
2	slices fresh ginger
5cm	piece lemon grass stem, halved lengthways

Peel and devein prawns. Finely chop prawns, salmon, green onions and chilli, combine with coriander and sesame oil. Lay 16 gow gee wrappers on workbench, divide seafood mixture between them. Brush edges with a little water, top with remaining wrappers, press edges together to seal; set aside.

Combine remaining ingredients in a saucepan, bring to a gentle simmer, cook for 5 minutes or until peas are tender. Scoop out garlic, ginger and lemon grass.

Meanwhile, bring a frying pan of water to boil, add half the gow gees, simmer for 2 minutes or until filling has heated through, remove and drain. Repeat with remaining gow gees. Place gow gees into shallow serving bowls and spoon over peas and stock.

NB: Gow gee wrappers are similar to wonton wrappers, without the egg. They are available from Asian food stores, some delicatessens and health food stores. If unavailable, use wonton wrappers. Gow gees can be assembled several hours ahead and stored in the refrigerator. Supermarkets sell homemade-style fish stock in Tetra packs.

serves 4

When buying fresh peas, choose small, waxy, plump, bright-green pods for the best flavour. The weight of unshelled peas you purchase should be almost three times the weight of shelled peas you require. Peas are at their sweetest when picked, so eat within two to three days.

In ancient Egypt, the pharaohs considered mushrooms to be such a delicacy that a royal decree was passed to forbid their consumption except at royal feasts. Later, Julius Caesar passed similar laws to prevent all but the privileged from eating them.

mushroom soup
with roasted capsicum and fennel

per serving 4.4g fat; 680kJ

2	medium (400g) red capsicums
1 tbsp	olive oil
2	small bulbs (250g) baby fennel, chopped
900g	button mushrooms, sliced
35g	(¼ cup) plain flour
1.5 litres	(6 cups) chicken stock
80ml	(⅓ cup) buttermilk

Quarter capsicums, remove seeds and membranes. Roast under grill or in very hot oven, skin side up, until skin blisters and blackens. Cover capsicums with plastic or paper for 5 minutes; peel away skin, chop.

Heat oil in large pan, cook fennel and mushrooms 2 minutes. Add flour and cook, stirring, 2 minutes. Stir in stock and simmer, covered, 20 minutes or until mushrooms are tender. Blend or process soup in batches until pureed.

Just before serving, reheat soup in pan, stir in buttermilk, cook until heated through. Top soup with roasted capsicum, and fennel leaves, if desired.

serves 6

andalusian **gazpacho**

per serving 0.7g fat; 127kJ

1	slice white bread
5	small (650g) tomatoes, peeled, seeded, coarsely chopped
1/2	medium (100g) green capsicum, coarsely chopped
1/2	small (50g) Spanish onion, coarsely chopped
1	(130g) Lebanese cucumber, peeled, seeded, coarsely chopped
60ml	(1/4 cup) red wine vinegar
2	small cloves garlic, crushed
160ml	(2/3 cup) tomato juice
2 tsps	olive oil
2 tbsps	chopped Lebanese cucumber, extra
2 tbsps	chopped Spanish onion, extra
2 tbsps	chopped green capsicum, extra
2 tbsps	chopped tomatoes, extra

Remove crusts from bread; discard crusts.

Blend or process bread, tomatoes, capsicum, onion, cucumber, vinegar, garlic, juice and oil until smooth. Strain tomato mixture through a coarse strainer over a large bowl. Refrigerate, covered, until cold.

Divide gazpacho between 8 x 80ml (1/3-cup) capacity shot glasses. Garnish with combined remaining ingredients.

serves 8

"The greatest dishes are very simple dishes."
ESCOFFIER

Under-ripe tomatoes should be left at room temperature to ripen and develop colour. All tomatoes should be taken out of the refrigerator at least half an hour before use.

roasted pumpkin and tomato soup with smoked almonds

per serving 7.7g fat; 1574kJ

2.5kg	Queensland Blue pumpkin
3	small (390g) ripe tomatoes, halved
2	large (600g) Spanish onions, finely chopped
2	cloves garlic, crushed
60g	(¼ cup) tomato paste
200g	(1 cup) brown rice
2 litres	(8 cups) chicken or vegetable stock
40g	(¼ cup) smoked almonds, coarsely chopped

Cut pumpkin into 2cm pieces.

Place pumpkin and tomatoes in large baking dish; spray with cooking oil spray. Bake in a moderately hot oven (200°C) about 20 minutes or until lightly browned.

Heat large, lightly oiled saucepan; cook onions and garlic, stirring, until onions are soft. Stir in paste, rice and stock; bring to boil, simmer, uncovered, about 30 minutes or until rice is tender.

Divide pumpkin and tomato among serving bowls; top with soup. Sprinkle with almonds to serve.

serves 6

seafood laksa

per serving 4.9g fat; 1037kJ

500g	small black mussels
250g	white fish fillets
1	medium (150g) onion, chopped
2 tsps	grated fresh ginger
1 tbsp	laksa paste
160ml	(2/3 cup) light coconut milk
1 litre	(4 cups) fish or chicken stock
500ml	(2 cups) water
150g	pad thai noodles
1 tbsp	lime juice
1/4 cup	torn fresh coriander leaves

Remove beards from mussels. Chop fish coarsely.

In a large saucepan, combine onion, ginger, laksa paste, coconut milk, stock and water, bring to boil. Add mussels, fish and noodles; simmer uncovered for about 5 minutes or until noodles are tender. Stir in juice, sprinkle with coriander.

NB: Squeezed lime juice and grated ginger are available from supermarkets. Pad thai noodles are available from supermarkets and specialist Asian food stores.

serves 4

When purchasing mussels, ensure they are firmly closed and have a pleasant sea smell. After cooking, the mussels should be open; discard any that are not.

mexican black bean soup
with lamb

per serving 7g fat; 1408kJ

400g	(2 cups) dried black beans
2.5 litres	(10 cups) water
400g	whole piece boneless lamb shoulder, halved
1	small (200g) leek, finely chopped
1	small (70g) carrot, finely chopped
375ml	(1½ cups) lamb or beef stock
1 tbsp	olive oil
3	cloves garlic, crushed
1	small (100g) Spanish onion, finely chopped
1	small (150g) red capsicum, finely chopped
2 tsps	ground cumin
250ml	(1 cup) lime juice
80ml	(⅓ cup) dry sherry
60ml	(¼ cup) balsamic vinegar
1	medium (190g) tomato, seeded, chopped
1 tbsp	salt

Cover beans with cold water in large bowl; stand overnight.

Drain the beans, then rinse under cold water; drain again. Bring 2 litres (8 cups) of the water to boil in large pan. Add lamb; simmer, covered, about 1½ hours or until tender. Strain lamb over medium bowl; reserve liquid. Place cooled lamb in separate large bowl; using fork, shred finely.

Return reserved cooking liquid to same pan with beans, leek, carrot, stock and remaining 500ml (2 cups) water. Bring to boil; simmer, uncovered, about 1 hour or until beans are tender. Remove from heat.

Heat oil in small pan; cook garlic, onion, capsicum and cumin, stirring, until onion is soft. Add to bean mixture with juice, sherry, vinegar, tomato, salt and shredded lamb.

Blend or process half the bean soup, in batches, until almost smooth; return to same pan with remaining soup and simmer until heated through.

NB: Soup can be made a day ahead. Cover; refrigerate overnight.

serves 6

Dried black beans are also called turtle beans; these full-flavoured dried beans bear no resemblance to the fermented soy beans, also known as black beans, that are commonly used in Chinese cooking.

sesame seed rolls

per roll 2.4g fat; 552kJ

30g	fresh yeast
2 tsps	sugar
250ml	(1 cup) lukewarm water
450g	(3 cups) plain flour
240g	(1½ cups) wholemeal plain flour
185g	(1½ cups) soy flour
1 tbsp	salt
560ml	(2¼ cups) lukewarm water, extra
1 tbsp	milk, for glazing
2 tbsps	sesame seeds

Combine yeast with sugar, stir until creamy. Add the water, cover with plastic wrap, stand 10-15 minutes or until mixture becomes a little foamy. Sift flours and salt into a large bowl, return wholemeal husks to the bowl, make a well in the centre, add yeast mixture and the extra water, mix well with hands or wooden spoon. Mixture should be heavy and sticky. Scrape down inside of bowl, cover with plastic wrap, stand for 1 hour or until mixture has doubled in bulk.

Turn dough onto a floured surface, divide in half for easier handling. Knead each half for 5 minutes or until dough is smooth and elastic. Divide each half into 12 equal pieces. Knead each piece until smooth and round in shape. Place 3cm apart on baking trays lined with baking paper. Stand, uncovered, for 15 minutes or until dough has doubled in bulk.

Brush tops with milk, sprinkle with sesame seeds. Bake in moderately hot oven (200°C) for 20 minutes or until golden brown. Serve hot, or cool on a wire rack.

NB: Stand the yeast and the dough in a warm place, such as a sunny corner, but not in the oven, which is too hot.

makes 24

pitta bread chips

per serving 2.4g fat; 692kJ

4	pieces pitta bread
	Cooking oil spray
2 tbsps	lemon pepper

Cut pitta bread into quarters, split quarters open into two pieces. Spray pitta bread with cooking oil spray, sprinkle with lemon pepper, and crisp in a hot oven (220°C) for a few minutes or until golden brown.

serves 6

caramelised onion toasts

per serving 13g fat; 949kJ

2 tbsps	olive oil
3	medium (450g) onions, sliced
2	cloves garlic, crushed
2 tsps	fennel seeds
4	slices stale sourdough bread, lightly toasted
40g	(⅓ cup) grated gruyère cheese
⅓ cup	chopped fresh parsley

Preheat oven to moderate (180°C). Heat oil in a non-stick pan, cook onions, garlic and fennel seeds over low heat for 15 minutes or until caramelised. Spoon onion mix over toast, sprinkle with cheese. Place onion toasts in a baking dish. Bake for 15 minutes or until cheese melts. Place onion toasts onto serving plates. Sprinkle with parsley.

serves 4

smoked cheddar damper

per serving 7.7g fat; 1230kJ

375g	(2½ cups) self-raising flour
1 tbsp	cracked black pepper
30g	butter
⅓ cup	chopped fresh parsley
60g	(½ cup) grated smoked cheddar cheese
180ml	(¾ cup) skim milk
80ml	(⅓ cup) water

Combine flour and pepper in a large bowl, rub in butter. Stir in parsley and cheese, then stir in milk and water. Turn dough onto a floured surface, knead until just smooth. Place on a baking tray lined with a sheet of baking paper, press into a 15cm round. Brush dough with a little extra milk, bake in moderate oven (180°C) 40 minutes or until damper sounds hollow when tapped.

serves 6

sesame seed rolls

caramelised onion toasts

smoked cheddar damper

pitta bread chips

stir-fries

stir-fried
leafy chinese greens

per serving 8.3g fat; 804kJ

1 tbsp	peanut oil
200g	Swiss brown mushrooms, sliced
900g	Chinese cabbage, chopped
340g	baby bok choy, chopped
4	green onions, chopped
1 tbsp	soy sauce
2 tbsps	oyster sauce
1 tsp	sesame oil
1 tsp	sesame seeds
3 cups	steamed white rice

Heat peanut oil in wok or large pan; stir-fry mushrooms 1 minute. Add cabbage and bok choy, stir-fry until just wilted. Stir in onions, sauces and sesame oil; stir-fry until well combined and heated through. Sprinkle with sesame seeds. Serve immediately with rice.

serves 4

As the name implies, baby bok choy is the smaller of the two bok choy varieties. It is milder in flavour than its more mature relative, but is equally excellent in stir-fries; both the stems and leaves of baby bok choy are edible.

mango chicken stir-fry

per serving 14.4g fat; 1704kJ

2 tbsps	vegetable oil
2	(340g) chicken breast fillets, thinly sliced
1	medium (170g) Spanish onion, sliced
1	small (150g) red capsicum, sliced
80ml	(1/3 cup) dry white wine
1	clove garlic, crushed
1	small red chilli, finely chopped
1	small (300g) mango, peeled, sliced
2 tbsps	shredded fresh basil leaves
60g	baby rocket leaves

"Appetite comes with eating; the more one has, the more one would have."

FRENCH PROVERB

Heat half the oil in a wok, stir-fry chicken over high heat 2 minutes or until golden brown, remove from wok. Heat remaining oil in wok, stir-fry onion and capsicum 2 minutes or until softened. Add wine, garlic and chilli, bring to boil. Add chicken and mango, stir-fry until warmed through. Remove from heat, stir in basil and rocket.

serves 2

tomato pasta stir-fry

per serving 12.4g fat; 2082kJ

400g	dried flat pasta
3	cloves garlic, crushed
125g	sliced prosciutto, chopped
8	medium (600g) egg tomatoes, roughly chopped
1½ tbsps	balsamic vinegar
¼ cup	chopped fresh parsley
¼ cup	shredded fresh basil
40g	(¼ cup) pine nuts, toasted

Cook pasta according to instructions on the packet. Combine garlic and prosciutto in a non-stick frying pan, stir-fry over low heat for 2 minutes or until browned. Add tomatoes, stir-fry over high heat for 2 minutes or until soft. Add pasta, vinegar, parsley and basil, stir-fry for 2 minutes or until heated through. Serve sprinkled with pine nuts.

serves 4

sugar snap and snow peas
with tofu and pistachios

per serving 14.2g fat; 1211kJ

2 tsps	peanut oil
500g	firm tofu, chopped
35g	(¼ cup) pistachios
2	cloves garlic, crushed
2	red Thai chillies, seeded, chopped
2 tsps	grated fresh ginger
400g	sugar snap peas
400g	snow peas
60ml	(¼ cup) sweet chilli sauce

Heat half the oil in a wok; stir-fry tofu and nuts, in batches, until lightly browned, remove from wok. Heat remaining oil in same wok, stir-fry garlic, chillies and ginger until fragrant. Add sugar snap and snow peas to wok; stir-fry until just tender. Return tofu and nuts to wok, add sauce; stir-fry, tossing to combine ingredients.

serves 4

chicken
with coriander and cashews

per serving 12.5g fat; 1296kJ

700g	chicken breast fillets, thinly sliced
1/4 cup	chopped fresh coriander leaves
2	red Thai chillies, seeded, finely chopped
1 tsp	sesame oil
2	cloves garlic, crushed
2 tsps	peanut oil
80ml	(1/3 cup) rice vinegar
60ml	(1/4 cup) sweet chilli sauce
1 tbsp	lime juice
35g	(1/4 cup) raw cashews, toasted
40g	(2/3 cup) snow pea sprouts
40g	(2/3 cup) snow pea tendrils

Combine chicken, coriander, chillies, sesame oil and garlic in large bowl, cover; refrigerate 3 hours or overnight.

Heat peanut oil in wok; stir-fry chicken mixture in batches, until browned and cooked through. Return all chicken mixture to wok. Add vinegar, sauce and juice; stir-fry until sauce boils. Add cashews; stir-fry until combined with chicken mixture. Just before serving, gently toss sprouts and tendrils with chicken mixture.

serves 4

"Food for thought is no substitute for the real thing."

WALT KELLY

lamb,
spinach and fetta stir-fry

per serving 13.9g fat; 1310kJ

1 tsp	olive oil
1	small (100g) Spanish onion, cut into thin wedges
1	clove garlic, crushed
150g	lamb backstrap fillet (eye of loin), thinly sliced
10	cherry tomatoes, halved
60g	baby spinach leaves
15g	fetta cheese

Heat oil in a non-stick frying pan, stir-fry onion and garlic until soft, remove from pan. Stir-fry lamb until brown, remove from pan. Stir-fry tomatoes until soft. Return onion and lamb to pan with spinach and cheese, stir-fry until warmed through.

Serve with rice, if desired.

serves 1

pork and hokkien noodle stir-fry

per serving 14.7g fat; 1829kJ

500g	fresh hokkien noodles
2 tsps	peanut oil
1 tbsp	grated fresh ginger
4	cloves garlic, crushed
1 tsp	sambal oelek
8	green onions, cut into 4cm lengths
200g	baby bok choy leaves
250g	Chinese barbecued pork, sliced
125ml	(½ cup) chicken stock
1 tbsp	ketjap manis

Chinese barbecued pork is available from Asian food stores. Ketjap manis is an Indonesian sweet soy sauce. As an alternative, use soy sauce with a small amount of brown sugar added.

Rinse noodles under hot water to separate them. Heat oil in a frying pan or wok, stir-fry ginger, garlic and sambal oelek 1 minute. Add onions and bok choy, stir-fry 1 minute. Add noodles, pork, stock and ketjap manis, stir-fry until heated through.

serves 4

"Eating well gives a
spectacular joy to life and
contributes immensely to goodwill
and happy companionship."

ELSA SCHIAPARELLI

stir-fried choy sum

per serving 12.4g fat; 601kJ

500g	choy sum leaves
1 tbsp	peanut oil
1	clove garlic, crushed
2 tsps	sesame seeds
½ tsp	cumin seeds
1 tsp	black mustard seeds
2 tsps	fish sauce
1 tbsp	lemon juice

Trim and discard roots from choy sum. Cut the leaves from the stems, cut stems into 4cm lengths. Heat oil in a wok or frying pan. Cook garlic and seeds, stirring, over heat 1 minute. Add choy sum stems, stir-fry 2 minutes. Add leaves, stir-fry until softened. Stir in fish sauce and lemon juice.

serves 2

This recipe for choy sum is ideal to serve on its own or as an accompaniment to grilled or stir-fried meat, chicken and seafood, or with plain rice.

pork and snow pea stir-fry

per serving 14.3g fat; 1135kJ

1 tbsp	olive oil
1	large (300g) Spanish onion, cut into thin wedges
400g	pork fillet, sliced
90g	(⅓ cup) tikka sauce
200g	snow peas
60g	snow pea sprouts
2 tbsps	low-fat plain yogurt

Heat oil in a wok, stir-fry onion over high heat for 1 minute, push to one side. Add pork, stir-fry for 2 minutes or until lightly browned. Add tikka sauce and snow peas, stir-fry for 1 minute or until snow peas are tender. Remove from heat, stir in sprouts and yogurt. Serve with rice or noodles.

serves 4

Tikka sauce is an Indian-style curry sauce available from supermarkets and delicatessens.

chermoula lamb
with tabouleh

per serving 14.3g fat; 1462kJ

600g	trim lamb eye of loin, thinly sliced
½ cup	chopped fresh parsley
1 tbsp	lemon rind
1 tbsp	lime rind
1 tbsp	lemon juice
1 tbsp	lime juice
2 tsps	ground turmeric
1 tsp	ground cayenne pepper
1 tbsp	ground cumin
1 tbsp	ground coriander
1	medium (170g) Spanish onion, finely chopped

tabouleh

55g	(⅓ cup) burghul
3 cups	firmly packed fresh flat-leaf parsley, coarsely chopped
¼ cup	coarsely chopped fresh mint leaves
3	medium (570g) tomatoes, chopped
1	medium (150g) onion, chopped
1	green onion, finely chopped
80ml	(⅓ cup) chicken stock
80ml	(⅓ cup) lemon juice

Combine all ingredients in large bowl, cover; refrigerate 3 hours
or overnight.

Heat oiled wok, stir-fry lamb mixture, in batches, until browned and
cooked as desired. Serve with tabouleh.

Tabouleh: Cover burghul with cold water, stand 15 minutes. Drain, press
as much water as possible from burghul. Place burghul in large bowl. Add
remaining ingredients to bowl, mix gently until combined.

serves 4

noodle and prawn chermoula

per serving 6.3g fat; 1194kJ

1kg	(40) medium uncooked prawns
150g	dried rice vermicelli
1 tbsp	olive oil
5	medium (950g) tomatoes, peeled, seeded, sliced

chermoula

2 tbsps	firmly packed fresh coriander leaves
2 tbsps	firmly packed fresh flat-leaf parsley
2 tbsps	lemon juice
1	birdseye chilli, seeded, chopped
1	clove garlic, chopped
1 tsp	ground cumin
1/2 tsp	sweet paprika
1/2 tsp	ground coriander

Shell and devein prawns, leaving tails intact. Combine prawns with chermoula in medium bowl. Cover; refrigerate 3 hours or, preferably, overnight. Place vermicelli in medium heatproof bowl, cover with boiling water, stand only until just tender; drain. Heat oil in wok or large pan, stir-fry prawns until cooked through; stir in tomatoes. Serve with vermicelli.

Chermoula: Blend or process all ingredients until almost pureed.

serves 4

Chermoula is just one of the many Moroccan flavours that have crept into today's kitchen. Used as a marinade or a sauce, like salsa or masala, it is made of herbs and spices according to the taste of the individual cook, but usually contains fresh coriander, cumin and paprika.

potato gnocchi
with lemon grass and shiitake broth

per serving 2.3g fat; 768kJ

1kg	pink-eye potatoes
2	eggs, lightly beaten
1	egg white, lightly beaten
75g	(½ cup) plain flour
½ tsp	ground nutmeg

lemon grass and shiitake broth

¼ cup	thinly sliced lemon grass
½ tsp	ground black pepper
100g	shiitake mushrooms, sliced
750ml	(3 cups) vegetable stock
2 tsps	chopped palm sugar
1	birdseye chilli, seeded, finely chopped
2 tsps	fish sauce

Boil, steam or microwave unpeeled potatoes until tender; cool slightly, peel. Mash potatoes, press through a fine sieve. Combine potato with remaining ingredients, refrigerate 30 minutes. Roll tablespoons of mixture into oval shapes. Place a piece of gnocchi in the floured palm of your hand, roll the back of a fork across gnocchi to make indentations. Toss gnocchi lightly in flour. Repeat with remaining gnocchi. Bring large pan of water to boil, add gnocchi in batches, cook 1 minute or until they float, remove with slotted spoon. Serve with lemon grass and shiitake broth.

Lemon grass and shiitake broth: Combine all ingredients in large pan, bring to boil, simmer, uncovered, 15 minutes or until reduced by half.

serves 6

"Try to cook so that it will surprise a little, agreeably... and astonish slightly, without shocking."

JEAN MARIE AMAT

lemon basil rice with chicken

per serving 13.5g fat; 2678kJ

1 tsp	olive oil
½	medium (175g) leek, sliced
1	clove garlic, crushed
100g	(½ cup) long-grain rice
375ml	(1½ cups) chicken stock
1	small (130g) tomato, chopped
1 tsp	shredded lemon rind
¼ cup	small fresh basil leaves
85g	(½ cup) sliced cooked chicken breast

Heat oil in a small saucepan, cook leek and garlic over low heat, stirring, until lightly browned. Stir in rice, stock, tomato and lemon rind, cover, cook over low heat for 10 minutes or until rice is tender and stock is almost absorbed. Stir in basil. Serve with chicken.

serves 1

penne with leafy greens

per serving 14.2g fat; 2315kJ

20g	slivered almonds
200g	penne
2 tsps	olive oil
4	green onions, chopped
4	cloves garlic, crushed
125g	cherry tomatoes, halved
125ml	(½ cup) white wine
250ml	(1 cup) vegetable stock
2 tbsps	red wine vinegar
50g	baby spinach leaves
50g	baby rocket leaves
30g	low-fat fetta cheese

How much pasta to cook? The general rule is to allow 100g of dried pasta for each person as a main meal.

Spread almonds on a baking tray, bake in moderate oven (180°C) for 10 minutes or until golden brown, set aside. Cook pasta according to instructions on packet, drain. Meanwhile, heat oil in a frying pan, add onions, garlic and tomatoes, stir over high heat 2 minutes. Add wine, cook until reduced by half. Add stock and vinegar, bring to boil, add pasta, cook until heated through. Remove from heat, stir in spinach and rocket. Serve sprinkled with almonds and cheese.

serves 2

spanish paella

per serving 14.9g fat; 2513kJ

12	medium (300g) uncooked king prawns
400g	blue-eye cod
8	black mussels
50g	chorizo sausage*
1 tbsp	olive oil
4	small (200g) chicken tenderloins
80ml	(1/3 cup) water
2	cloves garlic, crushed
1	medium (170g) Spanish onion, sliced
1	medium (200g) red capsicum, sliced
1/2 tsp	cayenne pepper
265g	(1 1/3 cups) short-grain rice
1	large (250g) tomato, chopped
150g	shelled fresh broad beans
500ml	(2 cups) chicken stock
250ml	(1 cup) water, extra
pinch	saffron threads
	Lemon wedges, to serve

Preheat oven to moderately hot (200°C). Peel and devein prawns, leaving tails intact. Cut cod into 5cm cubes. Remove beards from mussels. Thinly slice chorizo sausage.

Heat 2 tsps of the oil in a non-stick frying pan, cook prawns over high heat 1 minute each side until browned; remove. Cook cod for 1 minute each side until browned; remove. Cook sausage 1 minute until browned; remove. Cook chicken 1 minute each side until browned; remove. Heat the water in same pan, add mussels, cover with a lid or foil, cook 3 minutes or until opened; remove, reserve all pan juices.

Heat remaining oil in same pan, cook garlic, onion and capsicum over high heat, stirring, for 2 minutes or until softened. Add cayenne, stir over heat 1 minute. Transfer to a 30cm paella pan or a baking dish, stir in rice, tomato and broad beans.

Bring stock, extra water and saffron to boil in a saucepan, combine with rice in paella pan. Bake in moderately hot oven, uncovered, 10 minutes. Arrange prawns, cod, mussels, sausage and chicken over rice; top with pan juices. Cover with foil, bake 15 minutes without stirring or until rice is tender and most of the liquid has been absorbed. Serve with lemon wedges.

This is a Spanish sausage, smoked and heavily spiced. If unobtainable, use salami in its place.

serves 4

whole roast snapper
with lemon and currant pilaf

per serving 9.4g fat; 2054kJ

500g	baby beetroot, trimmed
1.5kg	whole snapper
2 tsps	olive oil
50g	baby rocket leaves

lemon and currant pilaf

500ml	(2 cups) chicken stock
1 tbsp	grated lemon rind
200g	(1 cup) long-grain rice
100g	(2/3 cup) dried currants

Place beetroot in a lightly oiled ovenproof dish, bake in hot oven (220°C) for 15 minutes or until tender. Peel, grate coarsely. Cut 3 shallow slashes across fish on both sides. Fill cavity with lemon and currant pilaf. Brush with oil, place into a large, lightly oiled ovenproof baking dish. Bake, uncovered, in moderately hot oven (200°C) 30 minutes or until fish is cooked. Serve with beetroot and rocket.

Lemon and currant pilaf: Combine stock and rind in large, heavy-based pan, bring to boil, add rice, reduce heat to low, cover; simmer for about 15 minutes or until liquid is absorbed and rice is tender. Stir in currants.

serves 4

spinach and parsley lasagne

per serving 9.6g fat; 1376kJ

1	large (180g) Spanish onion, chopped
2	cloves garlic, crushed
1kg	extra lean minced beef
125ml	(½ cup) dry red wine
4	medium (760g) tomatoes, chopped
60ml	(¼ cup) tomato paste
2 tbsps	chopped fresh oregano
½ cup	chopped fresh parsley
2	bunches English spinach, trimmed
2	packets (750g) fresh lasagne sheets
600g	(3 cups) reduced-fat ricotta
2 tbsps	chopped fresh parsley, extra

Oil a shallow 23cm-square (14-cup capacity) ovenproof baking dish. Cook onion and garlic in large oiled pan, stirring, until onion is soft. Add mince; cook, stirring, until mince is browned. Add wine, bring to boil, stir in tomatoes and paste, simmer, uncovered, about 15 minutes or until mixture is thick; cool slightly. Stir in herbs; cool slightly. Boil, steam or microwave spinach until just wilted, drain, squeeze out water. Cut lasagne sheets to fit prepared baking dish. Place 2 sheets in dish. Spread with ¼ of the ricotta, ¼ of the mince mixture and ¼ of the spinach. Repeat layers 3 more times. Bake, covered, in moderate oven (180°C) about 45 minutes or until lasagne is tender. Serve sprinkled with extra parsley.

serves 10

roasted zucchini
buckwheat risotto with preserved lemon

per serving 3.1g fat; 1955kJ

6	**small (540g) green zucchini, coarsely chopped**
	Sea salt
	Freshly ground black pepper
1	**medium (150g) brown onion, finely chopped**
2	**cloves garlic, crushed**
200g	**(1 cup) arborio rice**
200g	**(1 cup) raw buckwheat**
250ml	**(1 cup) dry white wine**
1 litre	**(4 cups) hot vegetable stock**
50g	**preserved lemons, thickly sliced**
¼ cup	**finely chopped fresh garlic chives**

Place zucchini on lightly oiled oven tray, spray with cooking oil spray; sprinkle with salt and pepper, bake in hot oven (220°C) about 15 minutes or until zucchini is golden brown. Keep warm.

Heat a non-stick saucepan; cook onion and garlic, stirring, until onion is soft. Add rice, buckwheat and wine; cook over low heat, stirring, until wine is absorbed. Stir in 250ml (1 cup) stock; cook, stirring, until liquid is absorbed. Continue adding stock in 250ml (1-cup) batches, stirring until liquid is absorbed before next addition. Total cooking time should be about 35 minutes, or until rice and buckwheat are tender. Stir in zucchini, lemon and chives, before serving.

serves 4

vietnamese salad
with mint

per serving 7.1g fat; 757kJ

200g	rice vermicelli noodles
350g	beef rump steak, thinly sliced
6	cloves garlic, crushed
2 tbsps	fish sauce
1 tsp	grated fresh ginger
1/2	medium (300g) daikon
110g	(2 cups) snow pea sprouts
2 tsps	peanut oil
1/4 cup	chopped fresh Vietnamese mint
35g	(1/4 cup) unsalted roasted cashews
2	small red chillies, seeded, finely chopped

Fed to slaves building the Egyptian pyramids to keep them strong, garlic has been hailed as a cure for toothache, the flu, consumption, open wounds and, of course, is well known for its reputed powers in warding off evil, particularly those pesky blood-suckers.

Place noodles in heatproof bowl, cover with boiling water, stand 5 minutes; drain.

Combine beef, garlic, sauce and ginger in large bowl, mix well; cover, refrigerate 3 hours or overnight. Cut daikon into thin strips; combine in large bowl with snow pea sprouts.

Heat oil in wok or large pan, stir-fry beef mixture in batches until beef is browned and tender.

Combine beef mixture with vegetable mixture, noodles, mint, cashews and chilli.

serves 8

beetroot risotto
with sesame glass biscuits

per serving 3.1g fat; 1864kJ

500g	baby beetroot, trimmed
2	cloves garlic, peeled
1 litre	(4 cups) vegetable stock
125ml	(½ cup) red wine
2 tbsps	Grand Marnier
1	medium (200g) white onion, chopped
400g	(2 cups) arborio rice
2 tbsps	balsamic vinegar

sesame glass biscuits

2 tbsps	liquid glucose
45g	plain flour
90g	caster sugar
2 tbsps	sesame seeds, toasted

Combine beetroot and garlic in oiled baking dish. Roast in hot oven (220°C) 25 minutes or until beetroot is tender. Cool, peel, chop beetroot and garlic. Blend or process until almost smooth. Combine in medium pan with stock, wine and Grand Marnier, bring to boil, keep hot. Add onion to large heated oiled pan; cook, stirring, until soft. Add rice, stir until well combined. Stir 160ml (⅔ cup) hot stock mixture into rice; cook, stirring, over low heat until liquid is absorbed. Continue adding stock mixture gradually, stirring until absorbed between additions. Total cooking time should be approximately 30 minutes or until rice is tender; stir in vinegar. Serve accompanied by sesame glass biscuits.

Sesame glass biscuits: Line a baking tray with a sheet of baking paper. Combine all ingredients in large bowl. Using wet hands, press mixture together to form a ball. Roll teaspoonfuls of mixture into balls; place 10cm apart on prepared tray, flatten slightly with wet hand. Bake in moderate oven (180°C) 7 minutes or until lightly browned; cool on tray. Makes about 24.

serves 6

spicy tomato and basil pasta

per serving 14.2g fat; 2236kJ

200g	dried pasta*
1 tbsp	olive oil
200g	button mushrooms, chopped
2	cloves garlic, crushed
400g	can crushed tomatoes
½ tsp	dried chilli flakes
2 tbsps	grated parmesan cheese
¼ cup	sliced fresh basil leaves

Cook pasta according to instructions on the packet. Heat oil in a frying pan, cook mushrooms and garlic over high heat, stirring, 2 minutes. Add undrained tomatoes and chilli, cook over low heat for 10 minutes or until reduced and thickened. Stir in pasta, cook until warmed through. Serve sprinkled with cheese and basil.

Use any shaped pasta of your choice.

serves 2

pumpkin fettuccine with crispy prosciutto

per serving 9.6g fat; 2195kJ

400g	fresh fettuccine
500g	jap pumpkin
4	rashers prosciutto
2 tsps	olive oil
2	cloves garlic, crushed
1	leek, sliced
400g	can crushed tomatoes
375ml	(1½ cups) chicken stock
100g	low-fat fetta cheese, crumbled
⅓ cup	roughly chopped fresh flat-leaf parsley

Cook fettuccine according to instructions on the packet, drain. Peel pumpkin, cut into thin slices. Boil, steam or microwave pumpkin until tender. Grill prosciutto until brown and crisp, drain on absorbent paper. Heat oil in a large frying pan, add garlic and leek, stir over medium heat for 2 minutes or until softened. Stir in undrained tomatoes and stock, simmer 3 minutes or until liquid has reduced by half. Add pasta, pumpkin, cheese and parsley, stir until all ingredients are heated through. Serve immediately, sprinkled with crumbled prosciutto.

serves 4

spaghettini with asparagus and walnut

per serving 10.6g fat; 1529kJ

16	stalks asparagus
2 tsps	olive oil
	Freshly ground black pepper
300g	spaghettini (or other pasta)
2 tsps	olive oil, extra
2	cloves garlic, thinly sliced
100ml	beef stock
1 tbsp	soy sauce
20g	walnuts, coarsely chopped
10g	grated parmesan cheese

Remove tough ends and peel lower part of asparagus, cut each stalk evenly into 3 pieces. Heat oil in saucepan, cook asparagus, season with pepper and set aside. Meanwhile, cook spaghettini according to directions on the packet. Heat extra oil in pan, cook garlic slowly until golden; add stock and soy sauce. Drain pasta, combine with garlic mixture. Place pasta in serving dish, top with asparagus and walnuts, sprinkle with parmesan and serve.

serves 4

pasta with fresh tuna and chilli dressing

per serving 13g fat; 2441kJ

500g	fresh tuna steaks
1 tbsp	olive oil
2 tbsps	lemon juice
2	cloves garlic, crushed
1 tsp	freshly ground black pepper
400g	bavette pasta
2 tsps	olive oil, extra
1	medium (150g) onion, thinly sliced
2	small fresh chillies, finely chopped
2 tbsps	chopped fresh flat-leaf parsley

Combine tuna in a baking dish with oil, lemon juice, garlic and pepper, bake in moderate oven (180°C) for 15 minutes or until tuna is just cooked through. Cut tuna into small pieces. Meanwhile, cook pasta according to instructions on the packet, drain. Heat extra oil in a frying pan, add onion, stir over medium heat until softened. Add chillies, stir over heat 1 minute. Add tuna, pasta and parsley, stir over heat until combined.

serves 4

spicy tomato and basil pasta

spaghettini with asparagus and walnut

pumpkin fettuccine with crispy prosciutto

pasta with fresh tuna and chilli dressing

vegetarian

chickpea and zucchini tagine

per serving 9g fat; 2771kJ

	Cooking oil spray
1	medium (150g) onion, sliced
1	clove garlic, crushed
1 tsp	ground turmeric
1/2 tsp	ground cinnamon
1/2 tsp	ground ginger
600g	pumpkin, chopped
4	large (600g) zucchini, chopped
250g	yellow pattipan squash, chopped
1 litre	(4 cups) vegetable stock
1 tbsp	honey
150g	(3/4 cup) chopped prunes
2	300g cans chickpeas, rinsed, drained
1/3 cup	chopped fresh coriander leaves

lemon couscous

400g	(2 cups) couscous
500ml	(2 cups) boiling water
25g	(1/3 cup) flaked almonds
1 tbsp	grated lemon rind

Coat a frying pan with cooking oil spray, cook onion and garlic over medium heat, stirring, until soft. Add spices; stir until fragrant.

Add vegetables, stock, honey and prunes; simmer, covered, about 5 minutes or until vegetables are just tender. Stir in chickpeas, simmer until hot. Serve immediately with lemon couscous, sprinkled with coriander.

Lemon couscous: Place couscous in bowl; cover with water. Stand 5 minutes, fluff with a fork. Heat large pan, cook almonds, stirring, until lightly browned. Add rind and couscous, stir until hot.

serves 4

asparagus
with honey and mustard

per serving 0.3g fat; 294kJ

1	**bunch (220g) asparagus**
1 tbsp	**water**
1 tbsp	**honey**
1 tbsp	**mustard**
1 tbsp	**lime juice**

Put asparagus in a freezer bag with the water. Close bag and microwave on HIGH (100%) for 2 minutes or until just tender. Combine honey, mustard and juice, pour over asparagus to serve.

serves 2

roasted
garlic celeriac

per serving 10.6g fat; 885kJ

1	large (1.5kg) celeriac
2 tbsps	olive oil
1	large garlic bulb
1/3 cup	chopped fresh flat-leaf parsley
80ml	(1/3 cup) low-fat plain yogurt (optional)

Peel celeriac, cut into 3cm chunks. Toss in oil, lay on a baking tray covered with a sheet of baking paper. Place garlic bulb on baking tray. Bake in moderate oven (180°C) for 1 hour or until celeriac is tender and golden brown, turn occasionally. Cut garlic in half horizontally, squeeze pulp over celeriac, toss together with parsley. The celeriac can be served topped with yogurt, if desired.

serves 4

bombay potato masala

per serving 3.6g fat; 908kJ

1.5kg	potatoes
20g	butter
1	large (200g) onion, sliced
3	cloves garlic, crushed
1 tsp	yellow mustard seeds
2 tsps	garam masala
1 tsp	ground coriander
1 tsp	ground cumin
½ tsp	chilli powder
¼ tsp	ground turmeric
400g	can crushed tomatoes, undrained

Cut potatoes into wedges. Boil, steam or microwave potato wedges until just tender; drain.

Heat butter in large pan; cook onion and garlic, stirring, until onion is soft. Add seeds and spices; cook, stirring, until fragrant. Stir in tomatoes; cook, stirring, 2 minutes or until sauce thickens slightly. Add potatoes; gently stir until heated through. Serve immediately.

serves 6

Scottish preachers once warned parishioners to shun the potato because there was no mention of it in the Bible. Now one of the world's favourite vegetables, the potato is a low-kilojoule, low-sodium food, high in vitamins C and B6. Prolonged exposure to light will give potatoes a green tinge, rendering them poisonous if eaten in large amounts.

penne with
asparagus
and broad beans

per serving 3g fat; 1529kJ

500g	fresh asparagus
500g	penne
2 tsps	olive oil
3	cloves garlic, crushed
1	large (300g) Spanish onion, chopped
2	medium (240g) zucchini, sliced
500g	frozen broad beans, thawed, peeled
250ml	(1 cup) chicken or vegetable stock
80ml	(1/3 cup) lemon juice
2 tsps	chopped fresh lemon thyme leaves
2 tsps	chopped fresh oregano
1/4 cup	fresh flat-leaf parsley

Snap and discard coarse ends from asparagus, cut into 4cm lengths. Boil, steam or microwave asparagus until just tender; drain, rinse under cold water, drain well. Cook pasta in large pan of boiling water; boil, uncovered, until just tender; drain, keep warm. Heat oil in pan, cook garlic, onion and zucchini, stirring, until onion is soft. Add asparagus and remaining ingredients; stir until hot. Combine pasta with vegetable mixture; toss well and serve immediately.

serves 6

Asparagus is at its best, and cheapest, in spring. When buying, select firm, crisp spears with compact tips and tight scales. The thickness of spears has no bearing on tenderness. To store, trim the base and stand upright in a little water. Cover with plastic and refrigerate. Use within 2-3 days.

capellini with capers and olives

per serving 9.6g fat; 1318kJ

1kg	ripe tomatoes
1 tbsp	olive oil
2	cloves garlic, crushed
1	medium (200g) red capsicum, chopped
100g	kalamata olives, sliced, seeds removed
2 tbsps	baby capers
⅓ cup	sliced fresh basil leaves
200g	dried capellini pasta
40g	shaved parmesan cheese (optional)

Cover tomatoes with boiling water, stand 2 minutes, drain, peel. Chop tomatoes roughly. Heat oil in a frying pan, cook garlic and capsicum, stirring, 1 minute. Add tomatoes, cover, cook over medium heat for 10 minutes or until tomato and capsicum have softened, stirring occasionally. Stir in olives, capers and basil. Meanwhile, cook pasta according to instructions on the packet, drain. Combine pasta with tomato sauce, serve sprinkled with cheese, if desired.

NB: Capellini is like a fine spaghetti. If unavailable, use 400g of your favourite shaped pasta.

serves 4

Guest Chef
Genee Wilner *Private Chefs, Inc.*

carrot and dill rosti

per serving 4.8g fat; 574kJ

60ml	(¼ cup) light sour cream
1 tsp	ground cumin
1 tbsp	chopped fresh dill
5	medium (600g) carrots, grated
1	egg, lightly beaten
1	egg white, lightly beaten
50g	(⅓ cup) plain flour

Combine sour cream, cumin and dill in small bowl. (Can be prepared up to a day ahead. Cover and refrigerate overnight.)

Combine carrot, egg, egg white and flour in large bowl. Cook ¼-cup measures of carrot mixture, in batches, on heated oiled barbecue plate, until rostis are browned both sides. Serve rostis with the sour cream mixture.

serves 4 (makes 12)

black and white garlic dip

per serving 9.8g fat; 509kJ

400g	soft or medium tofu
60ml	(1/4 cup) extra virgin olive oil
60ml	(1/4 cup) lemon juice
2	cloves garlic, crushed
1/4 tsp	sea salt
1 tbsp	baby capers
40g	(1/4 cup) chopped black olives

Combine tofu, oil, juice, garlic and salt in a food processor or blender, blend until smooth. Stir in capers and olives. Serve with water crackers or Lebanese bread.

serves 8 (makes about 1 1/2 cups)

Guest Chef
Tiffany Brown

Private Chefs, Inc.

silken tofu with
green pawpaw and carrot salad

per serving 3.7g fat; 721kJ

2	350g blocks firm silken tofu
1	small (650g) green pawpaw, peeled, halved, seeded, coarsely grated
2	small green chillies, seeded, chopped
1/3 cup	fresh coriander leaves
80ml	(1/3 cup) fresh lime juice
2 tbsps	shaved palm sugar
1 tbsp	finely chopped fresh lemon grass
3	kaffir lime leaves, shredded
2	medium (240g) carrots, coarsely grated
60ml	(1/4 cup) salt-reduced soy sauce
1 tbsp	rice wine vinegar
2	green onions, thinly sliced

Halve each tofu block lengthways, divide tofu between four serving plates. Top with combined remaining ingredients.

serves 4

honey-glazed tofu

per serving 8.9g fat; 1705kJ

500g	extra-firm tofu
60ml	(1/4 cup) tamari (soy sauce)
60ml	(1/4 cup) rice wine vinegar
1/4 cup	grated fresh ginger
2	green onions, finely chopped
2 tsps	sesame oil
2 tsps	wasabi
60ml	(1/4 cup) honey
200g	(1 cup) white and wild rice mix
1	green onion, cut into thin strips, extra

Cut tofu into 2cm slices, lay out in a baking dish. Combine tamari, vinegar, ginger, onions, sesame oil and wasabi. Pour over tofu, refrigerate at least 4 hours, turning tofu occasionally. Remove tofu from marinade, reserve marinade. Heat a non-stick frying pan to medium, add tofu in a single layer, cook for 1 minute on each side or until browned and warmed through; remove. Add marinade and honey to pan, stir over heat until slightly thickened. Meanwhile, cook rice according to instructions on the packet. Spoon rice onto serving plates, top with tofu, spoon over honey glaze. Top with green onion strips.

serves 4

black and white garlic dip

silken tofu with green pawpaw and carrot salad

honey-glazed tofu

vegetable curry

per serving 10g fat; 2057kJ

1 tbsp	canola oil
2	medium (300g) onions, chopped
2 tbsps	curry powder
2 tbsps	flour
250ml	(1 cup) light coconut milk
750ml	(3 cups) vegetable stock
2	large (360g) carrots, thickly sliced
1	medium (200g) red capsicum, roughly chopped
400g	kumara, peeled, cut into 3cm cubes
150g	cauliflower florets
150g	broccoli florets
2 tbsps	chopped fresh mint
265g	(1⅓ cups) basmati rice

Heat oil in a large saucepan, cook onion over high heat, stirring, 2 minutes. Add curry powder and flour, stir over heat 30 seconds. Add coconut milk and stock, stir over heat until simmering. Add carrot, capsicum and kumara, simmer 5 minutes. Add cauliflower and broccoli, simmer further 5 minutes or until vegetables are tender, stir in mint. Meanwhile, cook rice according to instructions on the packet, serve with vegetable curry.

serves 4

Guest Chef

Andy Ennis

Private Chefs, Inc.

kipfler **potato salad**

per serving 1.8g fat; 450kJ

500g	kipfler potatoes
1½ tbsps	low-fat mayonnaise
1 tbsp	low-fat plain yogurt
2 tbsps	water
1 tsp	seeded mustard
2 tsps	baby capers
2 tbsps	roughly chopped fresh dill

Scrub unpeeled potatoes under cold running water until clean. Steam potatoes for 20 minutes or until just tender, rinse under cold water, drain, cool. Halve potatoes lengthways. Combine mayonnaise, yogurt, the water, mustard, capers and dill in a large bowl, add potatoes, toss gently until combined.

serves 4

"If they like it,
it serves four;
otherwise, six."

ELSIE ZUSSMAN

barbecued rosti
with mint vinaigrette capsicums

per serving 13.2g fat; 1262kJ

500g	sebago potatoes
500g	carrots
2	eggs, lightly beaten
50g	(⅓ cup) plain flour
3 tsps	cumin seeds

mint vinaigrette capsicums

4	medium (800g) red capsicums
2 tbsps	extra virgin olive oil
2 tbsps	red wine vinegar
1	clove garlic, crushed
2 tbsps	shredded fresh mint leaves

Peel potatoes and carrots, grate coarsely. Combine with eggs, flour and cumin seeds. Cook ¼-cup measures of mixture in batches on a heated oiled barbecue plate for 2 minutes on each side or until rostis are golden brown and cooked through. Serve rostis with mint vinaigrette capsicums.

Mint vinaigrette capsicums: Quarter capsicums, remove seeds. Grill capsicums, skin side up, until skin has blackened. Peel away skin, combine capsicums with oil, vinegar, garlic and mint.

serves 4 (makes 12)

Guest Chef
Cheong Liew
The Grange Restaurant

nanjing salad

per serving 0.4g fat; 517kJ

2	**(260g) Lebanese cucumbers**
3	**medium (360g) carrots**
1 tbsp	**salt**
80ml	**(1/3 cup) rice vinegar**
3	**(480g) blood oranges***
1/2	**large (1kg) pineapple**
1	**small red chilli, finely chopped**
1/4 cup	**finely chopped fresh mint**

Peel cucumbers, halve lengthways, scoop out seeds, slice thinly. Peel carrots, cut into thin straws, preferably using a mandolin slicer. Combine cucumber and carrot in a bowl with salt, stand 30 minutes. Add vinegar, stand 30 minutes. Drain on absorbent paper.

Peel oranges, remove pith. Cut down each side of the membrane between each segment, lift segment out, remove seeds. Peel pineapple, chop roughly.

Combine cucumber, carrot, orange and pineapple in a bowl with chilli and mint.

* Blood oranges are available in winter. At other times use navel oranges.

serves 4

green salad with asian dressing

per serving 14.4g fat; 936kJ

1/2	**Chinese cabbage, sliced thickly**
100g	**(2 cups) bean sprouts, trimmed**
80g	**(1 cup) snow pea sprouts**
300g	**snow peas, halved diagonally**
1	**small (150g) yellow capsicum, cut into thin strips**
1/3 cup	**fresh coriander leaves**
1/3 cup	**fresh mint leaves**
1/3 cup	**(50g) roasted peanuts**

asian dressing

1/4 cup	**(60ml) rice vinegar**
1 1/2 tbsps	**canola oil**
2 tbsps	**mirin**
1 tbsp	**light soy sauce**
1 tsp	**sesame oil**

Combine all ingredients in a large bowl. Add dressing, toss well.

Dressing: Combine all ingredients in a jar, shake well.

NB: This salad can be served as a main course or as an accompaniment. For a main course, it is great tossed with sliced Chinese barbecued pork, shredded barbecued chicken or sliced, cooked beef or lamb.

serves 4

"If you like good food, cook it yourself."

LI LIWENG

fried green tomatoes
with rocket salad

per serving 7.3g fat; 1164kJ

4	medium (760g) green tomatoes
340g	(2 cups) polenta
2 tbsps	finely grated parmesan cheese
1 tbsp	olive oil
40g	(¼ cup) pepitas, roasted
30g	baby rocket leaves
20g	lamb's lettuce*
60ml	(¼ cup) vegetable stock
1 tbsp	balsamic vinegar

Slice tomatoes thickly. Combine polenta and parmesan in small bowl; coat tomato in polenta mixture. Heat oil in large heavy-based pan; cook tomato, in batches, until lightly browned on both sides. Serve with pepitas, rocket and lettuce, drizzle with combined stock and vinegar.

* If lamb's lettuce is impossible to obtain, it can be substituted with baby spinach.

serves 6

peking noodles
with asian mushrooms and lemon grass

per serving 1.2g fat; 727kJ

500g	Peking noodles
1/4 cup	finely chopped fresh lemon grass
2 tsps	finely grated lime rind
1	large (300g) Spanish onion, sliced thinly
300g	pine mushrooms*
250g	pink oyster mushrooms
250g	yellow oyster mushrooms
150g	enoki mushrooms
1 tbsp	sweet chilli sauce
2 tbsps	oyster sauce
80ml	(1/3 cup) vegetable stock

Cook noodles in large pan of boiling water, about 5 minutes or until tender; drain.

Cook lemon grass, rind and onion in large oiled wok or large pan until onion is tender. Add mushrooms, stir-fry 1 minute. Stir in noodles, combined sauces and stock, stir-fry until sauce boils and thickens slightly.

A pine mushroom forms the base upon which the noodles are stacked in this dish. If pine mushrooms are unobtainable, you can substitute dried porcini mushrooms, available from most delicatessens.

serves 6

Picking a good mushroom at the supermarket means looking for a tight, firm body with a thick stem and a clean, whitish colour. Keep them in the brown paper bags provided and store them in the refrigerator for up to two weeks.

tandoori potato and pumpkin pizza

per serving 11g fat; 2248kJ

200g	(1 cup) yellow split peas, rinsed
2 tbsps	chopped fresh coriander leaves
1½ tbsps	canola oil
2 tsps	grated fresh ginger
1	medium (150g) onion, finely sliced
200g	peeled pumpkin, finely sliced
1	large (300g) potato, finely sliced
2 tbsps	dried tandoori spice mix
4	round pitta breads
60g	wild rocket leaves*
125ml	(½ cup) low-fat plain yogurt
2 tbsps	chopped fresh mint leaves

Place split peas in medium pan, cover well with water, bring to boil, reduce heat to low; cook, uncovered, 45 minutes or until tender, drain (check water level occasionally). Blend or process until smooth; transfer to a bowl, stir in coriander.

Preheat oven to moderately hot (210°C). Combine oil, ginger, onion, pumpkin, potato and spice mix in a baking dish, bake 15 minutes or until tender.

Place pitta breads on oven trays, spread with split pea mixture, top with vegetables. Bake 15 minutes or until bases are crisp. Serve pizzas topped with rocket and drizzled with combined yogurt and mint.

NB: Split pea mixture can be made a day ahead.

* Look for these at greengrocers that stock gourmet lettuce. If unavailable, use baby rocket leaves instead.

serves 4

Yellow and green split peas are a variety of common garden pea that, once picked, has been peeled, split in half and dried. They do not keep their shape when cooked, so are most commonly used in soups or stews or, as here, to make a paste or puree.

roasted **root vegetables**

per serving 10g fat; 1712kJ

2 tsps	olive oil
6	baby carrots, peeled, halved
1	small (60g) parsnip, peeled, quartered lengthways
6	baby potatoes, halved
3	baby onions, halved
1	clove garlic, crushed
1 tbsp	rosemary leaves
1 tbsp	honey
2 tsps	seeded mustard
1 tbsp	lemon juice
2 tbsps	low-fat plain yogurt

Preheat oven to moderately hot (200°C). Heat oil in a baking dish on stove-top. Place carrots, parsnip, potatoes and onions in baking dish, cook over heat until lightly browned, turning occasionally. Remove from heat, stir in garlic, rosemary, honey and mustard. Transfer to oven, bake 20 minutes or until vegetables are tender. Drizzle with lemon juice, serve with yogurt.

Hint: Delicious served with grilled meat, chicken, fish or prosciutto.

serves 1

"Food is an important part of a balanced diet."
FRAN LEBOWITZ

spiced carrot salad

per serving 2.7g fat; 298kJ

4	large (720g) carrots
1	clove garlic, crushed
1/2 tsp	sweet paprika
1/2 tsp	ground cumin
2	birdseye chillies, seeded, chopped
2 tbsps	lemon juice
2 tsps	olive oil
1/4 tsp	sugar
2 tbsps	chopped fresh coriander leaves

Cut carrots into long, thin strips; boil, steam or microwave until just tender. Meanwhile, combine garlic, paprika, cumin, chillies, juice, oil and sugar in jar; shake well. Combine carrots with dressing and coriander in large bowl while hot; mix gently. Serve warm or cold.

serves 4

tomato salad with preserved lemons

per serving 10.8g fat; 740kJ

2	large (700g) red capsicums
300g	(2 cups) broad beans, peeled
1kg	firm ripe tomatoes, peeled, seeded, coarsely chopped
2 tbsps	lemon juice
1/2 tsp	ground cumin
1	clove garlic, finely chopped
2 tbsps	olive oil
100g	green olives
2 tbsps	chopped fresh flat-leaf parsley
1	red Thai chilli, seeded, finely sliced
1 tbsp	preserved lemon peel, thinly sliced

Quarter capsicums, remove seeds and membranes. Place on oven trays, skin side up; grill until skin blisters and blackens. Stand 5 minutes, peel. Chop coarsely. Cook beans until just tender.

Combine capsicum, beans, tomato, juice, cumin, garlic and oil in large bowl; mix well.

Stir in olives, parsley, chilli and lemon; toss gently. Stand 10 minutes before serving.

serves 4

potato and rocket salad with roasted almonds

per serving 12.7g fat; 896kJ

50g	(2/3 cup) flaked almonds
1kg	desiree potatoes
60g	low-fat fetta cheese
60g	low-fat ricotta cheese
60ml	(1/4 cup) extra virgin olive oil
1 1/2 tbsps	Dijon mustard
1 1/2 tbsps	tarragon vinegar
1 1/2 tbsps	water
2	cloves garlic, crushed
	Salt and pepper, to taste
100g	baby rocket leaves
100g	watercress

Preheat oven to moderately hot (200°C). Spread almonds on a baking tray, bake for 10 minutes or until lightly browned, stirring occasionally; set aside. Steam or boil whole potatoes for 15 minutes or until just tender; drain, cool in cold water. Drain potatoes again, cut into thick slices. Combine fetta and ricotta. Combine oil, mustard, vinegar, the water, garlic, salt and pepper in a bowl. Lay potato slices on a serving platter, drizzle with half the mustard dressing. Top with rocket and watercress, drizzle with remaining dressing. Sprinkle with crumbled fetta mixture and almonds.

NB: Almonds, potatoes, fetta mixture and dressing can all be prepared up to a day ahead. Assemble just before serving.

serves 8

"It takes four men to dress a salad: a wise man for the salt; a madman for the pepper; a miser for the vinegar; and a spendthrift for the oil."

ANONYMOUS

spiced carrot salad

potato and rocket salad with roasted almonds

tomato salad with preserved lemons

meat

beef and veal

beef, avocado
and white bean salad

per serving 6.6g fat; 842kJ

2 tsps	ground black pepper
600g	piece beef fillet
100g	baby rocket leaves
2	240g cans cannellini beans, drained
2 tsps	fresh lemon thyme leaves
1	medium (250g) avocado, thinly sliced
100g	fresh garlic chives
1	clove garlic, crushed
1 tsp	raw sugar
1 tbsp	lemon juice
60ml	(¼ cup) chicken stock

Press pepper onto beef. Heat oiled non-stick pan, cook beef, turning until browned all over. Place beef in baking dish, bake in hot oven about 10 minutes or until cooked as desired. Stand beef 5 minutes before slicing.

Serve beef with combined remaining ingredients.

serves 6

*Eating garlic can help keep mosquitoes away –
not to mention most other living creatures too!
It has been claimed, however, that chewing parsley
can help to eliminate "garlic breath".*

steak sandwich

per serving 8.3g fat; 1404kJ

400g	piece beef fillet
2 tbsps	cracked black peppercorns
2 tsps	finely grated lemon rind
6	small (780g) ripe tomatoes, halved
8	thick slices grain or brown bread, toasted
2 tbsps	low-fat plain yogurt
2 tsps	wholegrain mustard
30g	baby spinach leaves

Coat beef in peppercorns and rind. Cook beef in heated, oiled pan until browned all over and cooked as desired. Remove; stand beef, covered, 5 minutes.

Meanwhile, cook tomatoes in the same pan for 2 minutes on each side or until lightly browned and slightly softened.

Spread toasted bread with combined yogurt and mustard. Slice beef into 8 slices and serve immediately on bread with tomatoes and spinach.

serves 4

fillet steaks with capsicum pesto

per serving 8.1g fat; 986kJ

4	(600g) beef fillet steaks
2 tbsps	chopped fresh basil leaves

capsicum pesto

1	large (350g) red capsicum, seeded, quartered
40g	(1/4 cup) sun-dried tomatoes in oil, rinsed
2 tsps	grated fresh ginger
1 tsp	sugar

Cook beef on heated, oiled, barbecue plate until browned both sides and cooked as desired. Serve steaks topped with capsicum pesto and sprinkled with basil.

Capsicum pesto: Grill capsicum, skin side up, until blackened, cool. Peel away skin, chop capsicum roughly. Blend or process capsicum, sun-dried tomatoes, ginger and sugar.

serves 4

moroccan minted beef

per serving 7.6g fat; 830kJ

2 tsps   olive oil
750g   beef strips
1   large (200g) onion, sliced
2 tsps   ground cumin
1 tsp   grated lemon rind
400g   can crushed tomatoes
2 tbsps   slivered almonds, toasted
2 tbsps   shredded fresh mint leaves

Heat oil in a frying pan, cook beef in batches, over high heat, until browned all over, remove. Add onion, stir over heat until tender. Add cumin and rind, stir until fragrant. Add undrained tomatoes, simmer until thickened slightly, stir occasionally. Add beef, stir until heated through. Serve immediately, sprinkled with almonds and mint.

serves 6

Guest Chef
Andrew Skinner
The Ritz-Carlton, Sydney

veal medallions with pumpkin risotto

per serving 5.2g fat; 1726kJ

250g	peeled pumpkin, cut into 1cm cubes
2 tsps	olive oil
1	medium (150g) onion, finely chopped
200g	(1 cup) arborio rice
250ml	(1 cup) water
750ml	(3 cups) chicken stock
2	medium (380g) tomatoes, peeled, seeded, chopped
12	(240g) baby carrots
12	snow peas
12	asparagus spears
12	cauliflower florets
4	100g veal medallions
60ml	(¼ cup) madeira
180ml	(¾ cup) veal or beef stock

Boil or steam pumpkin until tender; drain, set aside. Heat oil in a medium saucepan, cook onion over medium heat, stirring, until tender. Stir in rice. Add water and ½ cup of chicken stock, stir over heat until liquid is absorbed. Add remaining chicken stock, ½ cup at a time, stir until absorbed between additions. Add pumpkin and tomato, stir until heated through.

Meanwhile, boil or steam carrots, snow peas, asparagus and cauliflower until tender; drain, keep warm.

Heat an oiled, non-stick frying pan, cook veal medallions over high heat for 1 minute on each side or until browned and cooked as desired, remove. Pour madeira into pan, then add veal stock; simmer, uncovered, until reduced by half. Serve vegetables and risotto with veal, drizzle with madeira sauce.

serves 4

melt-in-the-mouth veal shanks

per serving 1.5g fat; 721kJ

2	French-trimmed veal shanks*
1	large (500g) leek, sliced
2	cloves garlic, crushed
2 tbsps	chopped sun-dried tomatoes
1	large (180g) carrot, chopped
4	medium (760g) tomatoes, chopped
1/2	390g can pimentos, drained, chopped
125ml	(1/2 cup) red wine
250ml	(1 cup) chicken stock
1 tbsp	chopped fresh oregano
1 tbsp	baby capers

Combine veal shanks in a large saucepan with remaining ingredients; cover and cook over low heat for 1½ hours or until veal is very tender, stirring occasionally.

NB: You can serve this dish with the bone still in; however, as 1 shank is enough for 2 serves, you may prefer to remove the meat from the bones for easier serving.

Shanks are delicious served with boiled potatoes mashed with skim milk, salt and pepper.

* Ask your butcher to "French trim" the veal shanks for you. This means he will trim the bones and meat. Ask him especially to remove all visible fat.

serves 4

beef and ale with potato mash and mustard

per serving 7.4g fat; 1701kJ

500g	**beef round steak, coarsely chopped**
2	**small (160g) onions, roughly chopped**
2	**cloves garlic, crushed**
2	**large (360g) carrots, roughly chopped**
2 tbsps	**plain flour**
250ml	**(1 cup) light ale**
750ml	**(3 cups) beef stock**
800g	**potatoes, halved**
250ml	**(1 cup) skim milk**
2 tbsps	**seeded mustard**

Cook steak, in batches, in lightly oiled, large saucepan. Add onion, garlic and carrot; cook, stirring, until onion is soft. Stir in flour; cook 1 minute. Add ale and stock; simmer, covered, about 1 hour 15 minutes or until beef is tender.

Meanwhile, boil, steam or microwave potato until tender; drain. Mash potato with milk until almost smooth. Stir in mustard until just combined.

Serve beef with potato.

serves 4

"Food is our common ground, a universal experience."

JAMES BEARD

"After a good dinner one can forgive anybody, even one's own relations."

OSCAR WILDE

osso buco

per serving 9.3g fat; 1307kJ

1.5kg	(about 6) veal osso buco
	Plain flour
2 tbsps	olive oil
12	(300g) baby onions
4	cloves garlic, crushed
60g	(¼ cup) tomato paste
750ml	(3 cups) beef stock
250ml	(1 cup) red wine
400g	can crushed tomatoes
2	bay leaves
12	(240g) baby carrots

Remove and discard any excess fat from osso buco, dust with flour. Heat oil in a frying pan, add osso buco, cook until well browned all over. Transfer to a large saucepan with onions, garlic, tomato paste, stock, wine, undrained tomatoes and bay leaves. Simmer, covered, for 1 hour. Add carrots; cook, uncovered, further 30 minutes or until meat is very tender and sauce thickened; stir occasionally.

serves 6

mustard cabbage
and gourmet sausage hotpot

per serving 9.8g fat; 695kJ

	Olive oil spray
4	(350g) gourmet sausages
8	(200g) spring onions, halved
2	cloves garlic, crushed
2 tsps	cumin seeds
600g	cabbage, thickly sliced
750ml	(3 cups) chicken stock
2 tbsps	wholegrain mustard
3 tsps	fresh thyme leaves
2 tsps	brown sugar
300g	can butter beans

Heat a non-stick pan to medium, spray with olive oil spray. Cook sausages in pan for 10 minutes or until cooked through, turning occasionally; remove from pan. Add spring onions to pan juices, cook over medium heat for 3 minutes or until lightly browned, stirring occasionally. Add garlic and cumin, stir 1 minute. Add cabbage, stock, mustard, thyme and sugar, cover; cook over medium heat for 10 minutes or until spring onions and cabbage are tender. Cut sausages in half lengthways, add to pan with drained beans, cover, cook until heated through.

serves 4

pot-roasted
tangerine beef

per serving 4.6g fat; 1111kJ

3	medium (600g) tangerines or mandarins
1kg	beef topside
1	large (200g) brown onion, sliced
2 tsps	raw sugar
310ml	(1¼ cups) beef stock
60ml	(¼ cup) salt-reduced soy sauce
1 tbsp	grated fresh ginger
4	star-anise
1 tsp	Chinese five-spice powder
300g	dried rice noodles

Remove peel from tangerines, remove as much of the white pith as possible; slice thickly. Place peel on baking tray and bake in a slow oven for 30 minutes or until crisp and dry but not browned.

Place beef in heated, heavy-bottomed pot, cook until well browned all over. Add onion and cook for 2 minutes or until lightly browned, stir in sugar, stock, soy sauce, ginger, star-anise, five-spice powder and tangerine peel. Place lid on pot, simmer for 1½ hours or until beef is tender.

Add noodles to large pan of boiling water, cook according to directions on packet; drain.

Remove beef from pot, cover and keep warm. Bring sauce to boil, cook until slightly thickened and reduced by half. Slice beef, divide between serving plates with noodles and sauce.

serves 8

roasted vegetables with chilli jam

per serving 2.1g fat; 1959kJ

1	large (500g) kumara
2	medium (240g) zucchini
2	large (700g) yellow capsicums
4	medium (760g) vine-ripened tomatoes
2	large (360g) carrots
1/2	medium (800g) butternut pumpkin
2	medium (340g) Spanish onions

chilli jam

1	medium (150g) onion, chopped
2	cloves garlic, crushed
2 tsps	grated fresh ginger
4	large (1kg) tomatoes, seeded, chopped
1/4 cup	chopped fresh basil
125ml	(1/2 cup) red wine vinegar
80ml	(1/3 cup) dry sherry
2	birdseye chillies, seeded, chopped
165g	(3/4 cup) raw sugar

Peel and slice kumara into 1.5cm slices. Cut zucchini crossways into 3. Quarter capsicums, remove seeds and membranes. Halve tomatoes. Peel and halve carrots lengthways. Cut pumpkin into 2cm slices. Peel onions, cut into quarters.

Place vegetables on oven trays, spray with a little cooking oil spray. Bake, uncovered, in very hot oven (240°C) about 20 minutes or until browned. Turn vegetables, bake another 10 minutes or until browned and softened. Peel skin from capsicum. Serve vegetables immediately with chilli jam.

Chilli jam: Combine all ingredients in large pan, bring to boil, simmer 30 minutes or until thickened, stirring occasionally.

NB: Jam is best made a day ahead, for flavour.

serves 4

grilled baby eggplants

per serving 10g fat; 450kJ

4	baby eggplants
1 tbsp	olive oil
2 tsps	finely chopped preserved lemon
3 tsps	tarragon vinegar
2 tbsps	chopped fresh flat-leaf parsley

Cut eggplants in half lengthways. Brush cut side of each with oil. Heat a char-grill pan or frying pan. Place eggplants, cut side down, in pan, cook over medium-high heat for 2 minutes or until browned. Turn, cook 2 minutes or until tender. Transfer to a plate, spread cut side with preserved lemon. Drizzle with vinegar, sprinkle with parsley.

serves 2

Guest Chef

Genee Wilner

Private Chefs, Inc.

honey-glazed beetroot

per serving 4.5g fat; 1020kJ

8	medium (1.4kg) beetroot, trimmed
3	oranges
20g	butter
2 tsps	cornflour
60ml	(1/4 cup) honey

Preheat oven to moderately hot (200°C). Place unpeeled beetroot in a baking dish, bake for 45 minutes or until tender, allow to cool. Peel beetroot, cut into wedges. Peel the rind (not the pith) from one of the oranges, cut into very fine strips. Juice the oranges – you will need 160ml (2/3 cup). Melt butter in a frying pan, stir in cornflour, then orange juice and honey, stir over heat until simmering. Add beetroot wedges, continue stirring until wedges are coated with glaze. Serve at room temperature topped with orange rind strips.

serves 4

snake beans with almonds and prosciutto

per serving 5.8g fat; 385kJ

400g	snake beans
2 tsps	olive oil
1 tbsp	flaked almonds
1	small (80g) onion, finely chopped
1	clove garlic, crushed
1 tbsp	lemon juice
4	rashers prosciutto

Halve beans (or cut into short lengths for easier handling). Bring a frying pan of water to boil, cook beans for 2 minutes or until tender but not soft; drain. Heat half the oil in pan, cook almonds over medium heat for 2 minutes or until browned; remove. Heat remaining oil in pan, cook onion and garlic over medium heat, stirring, for 2 minutes or until soft.

Remove from heat, return beans to pan, with almonds and lemon juice, stir until combined.

Meanwhile, grill prosciutto for 1 minute on each side or until crisp, chop roughly. Add to beans.

NB: Serve snake beans wherever you would use regular beans, ie, in a stir-fry or as an accompaniment to meats, chicken and fish.

serves 4

roasted vegetables with chilli jam

honey-glazed beetroot

grilled baby eggplants

snake beans with almonds and prosciutto

lamb

moroccan lamb burger

per serving 7.5g fat; 1748kJ

400g	Trim Lamb round roast
1 tbsp	harissa paste
1 tbsp	lemon juice
2 tbsps	chopped fresh coriander root
2 tbsps	chicken stock
4	sourdough rolls or similar
1	butter lettuce
2	small (260g) vine-ripened tomatoes, thickly sliced
80ml	(1/3 cup) reduced-fat plain yogurt
30g	preserved lemons, chopped

Combine lamb, harissa, lemon juice, coriander and stock in small bowl Cover and refrigerate for 3 hours or overnight.

Remove lamb from marinade, discard marinade. Cook lamb on oiled barbecue bars until well browned all over and cooked as desired. Remove from barbecue, wrap in foil and leave to rest for 10 minutes.

While lamb is resting, slice each sourdough roll into 3, brush with a little olive oil and cook on oiled barbecue bars until lightly browned. Slice lamb and layer between sourdough with lettuce and tomato slices. Top with combined yogurt and preserved lemon.

NB: Harissa and preserved lemon are available from speciality food stores and delicatessens.

serves 4

"Let the stoics say what they please, we do not eat for the good of living, but because the meat is savoury and the appetite is keen."

RALPH WALDO EMERSON

tandoori lamb cutlets with grilled lemon

per serving 8.3g fat; 851kJ

200g	low-fat plain yogurt
1	medium (150g) onion, chopped
2 tbsps	lemon juice
2 tsps	vegetable oil
1 tbsp	chopped fresh ginger
3	cloves garlic, chopped
2 tsps	chilli powder
1 tsp	garam masala
1 tsp	ground cumin
1	tiny pinch tandoori coloured powder
8	large lamb cutlets
2	lemons, thickly sliced

Blend or process all ingredients, except cutlets and lemons, until pureed. Combine cutlets with pureed mixture in large bowl; cover, refrigerate overnight. Cook cutlets and lemon slices, in batches, on a heated, oiled grill pan (or grill or barbecue) until brown and tender.

serves 4

roast lamb with lemons and olives

per serving 13.3g fat; 1468kJ

1kg	boned leg of lamb
1	medium (140g) lemon, cut into eighths
160g	(1 cup) kalamata olives
10	cloves garlic, unpeeled
60ml	(¼ cup) chicken stock
60ml	(¼ cup) dry white wine
2 tbsps	finely chopped fresh oregano

Preheat oven to moderately slow (160°C). Remove fat from lamb, tie with string. Place lamb in shallow, large baking dish with lemon, olives and garlic. Pour stock and wine over lamb, sprinkle with oregano. Bake, uncovered, 1 hour or until cooked as desired.

serves 6

lamb and chickpea hotpot

per serving 13.7g fat; 2346kJ

1 tbsp	olive oil
400g	diced lean lamb
1 tsp	crushed garlic
370g	carton chunky Roma tomatoes and chilli
2 tsps	cumin seeds
1 tsp	ground turmeric
375ml	carton (1½ cups) chicken stock
150g	(½ can) chickpeas*
¼ cup	chopped fresh coriander
1 tbsp	lemon juice
200g	(1 cup) couscous

Heat oil in a non-stick frying pan, cook lamb and garlic for 3 minutes or until lamb has browned, stirring occasionally. Add tomatoes, cumin, turmeric, stock and chickpeas. Bring to boil, reduce heat to low, cook, covered, for 45 minutes or until lamb is tender. Stir in coriander and juice.

Meanwhile, combine couscous in a bowl with 250ml (1 cup) boiling water, cover, stand 10 minutes, fluffing couscous occasionally with a fork. Serve lamb with couscous.

NB: To make this recipe quick to prepare, use ready-diced lamb. Crushed garlic and lemon juice can be bought at the supermarket along with the other convenient ingredients. All you need to do is chop the coriander.

If preferred, use dried chickpeas: soak in water overnight; drain. Cover with water in a saucepan, bring to boil, cook on low heat for 1 hour; drain.

serves 3

"I like a cook who smiles out loud
when he tastes his own work.
Let God worry about your modesty.
I want to see your enthusiasm."
ROBERT FARRAR CAPON

lamb meatballs with onion jam

per serving 5.3g fat; 1153kJ

750g	minced lamb
70g	(1 cup) stale breadcrumbs
2	cloves garlic, crushed
2	small red chillies, chopped
2 tsps	grated lemon rind
2 tsps	ground cumin
2 tsps	ground coriander
2 tbsps	chopped fresh mint

onion jam

3	large (600g) onions, thinly sliced
180ml	(3/4 cup) brown malt vinegar
75g	(1/3 cup) raw sugar

Combine lamb, breadcrumbs, garlic, chilli, lemon rind, cumin, coriander and mint. Roll 1/4-cup measures of mixture into sausage shapes. Cook sausages on a heated, oiled barbecue until browned all over. Serve with onion jam.

Onion jam: Combine onions, vinegar and sugar in a medium saucepan, cook over low heat, uncovered, for 40 minutes or until mixture caramelises, stirring occasionally.

NB: Meatballs can be grilled instead of barbecued, if preferred.

serves 6

Use rubber gloves when chopping fresh chillies as they can burn your skin. Removing the seeds will lessen the heat level.

spring lamb salad with raspberries

per serving 5.4g fat; 1327kJ

120g	(2/3 cup) wild rice
500g	spring lamb fillets
200g	baby spinach leaves
1	small (100g) Spanish onion, thinly sliced
400g	fresh raspberries
2 tbsps	raspberry vinegar
1 tbsp	seeded mustard
1 tbsp	lemon juice
1 tbsp	dry white wine

Cook rice in pan of boiling water until tender; drain. Cook lamb in batches on heated, oiled barbecue or grill pan until cooked as desired. Cover lamb, rest 5 minutes; slice. Gently toss rice and lamb with spinach leaves, onion and raspberries. Drizzle with combined vinegar, mustard, juice and wine.

serves 4

Like most fruit, nectarines are high in nutrition and low in fat. As well as their vitamin C and fibre benefits, say naturopaths, nectarines are a good source of electrolytes in hot weather — it's no accident on mother nature's part that summer is prime season for them.

grilled lamb with nectarines

per serving 10.1g fat; 958kJ

4	**small (400g) ripe nectarines**
2 tbsps	**orange juice**
1 tbsp	**brown sugar**
8	**(600g) lean lamb cutlets**
1 tbsp	**olive oil**
1 tbsp	**fresh lemon thyme leaves**
	Freshly ground black pepper
2 tbsps	**fruit chutney**

Preheat grill to high. Halve and deseed unpeeled nectarines. Combine in a bowl with orange juice and sugar. Brush cutlets with oil, sprinkle with thyme and pepper. Grill nectarines, cut side up, until golden brown. Meanwhile, grill cutlets under high heat, for about 2 minutes on each side or until cooked to your liking. Spread cutlets with chutney, top with nectarines.

NB: Serve with 70g baby English spinach leaves, if desired.

serves 4

baby beetroots with
lamb and red wine

per serving 11.5g fat; 1484kJ

250g	lamb backstrap fillet (eye of loin)
1	clove garlic, crushed
2 tsps	chopped fresh rosemary
2 tsps	seeded mustard
8	baby beetroots
125ml	(½ cup) red wine
125ml	(½ cup) chicken stock

Preheat oven to moderately hot (200°C). Combine lamb in a bowl with garlic, rosemary and mustard, set aside. Trim leaves from beetroots, leaving a few intact. Leave the root intact. Cook in a saucepan of boiling water for 15 minutes or until soft; drain, cool slightly. To peel them, rub your fingers over the skin so that it slips off the beetroot.

Meanwhile, heat a non-stick frying pan to medium, cook lamb for 2 minutes on each side or until browned. Remove from heat, transfer lamb to a baking dish. Pour wine into frying pan, return to heat, add stock, bring to boil. Pour stock over lamb, bake for 10 minutes (for rare) or until lamb is cooked the way you like it. Serve beetroots with sliced lamb and cooking liquid.

serves 2

If you've only eaten vinegary canned beetroot, you won't believe a fresh beetroot is the same vegetable. Baby beetroot are never peeled before cooking; leave the root intact and trim the leaves, leaving about 4cm. If the leaves are young and fresh, they can be used too.

lamb cutlets
with chinese broccoli and chilli noodles

per serving 8.9g fat; 1113kJ

2	cloves garlic, crushed
1 tbsp	oyster sauce
60ml	(1/4 cup) hoisin sauce
2 tsps	sweet chilli sauce
12	lamb cutlets

chinese broccoli and chilli noodles

420g	packet thin fresh egg noodles
2 tsps	peanut oil
1	medium (200g) red capsicum, thinly sliced
1	clove garlic, sliced
1/2 tsp	finely chopped fresh ginger
500g	Chinese broccoli, chopped
60ml	(1/4 cup) mild sweet chilli sauce
1 tbsp	light soy sauce

Combine all ingredients in bowl; cover, refrigerate 3 hours or overnight. Cook cutlets, in batches, on heated, oiled grill pan (or grill or barbecue) until browned on both sides and tender. Serve cutlets topped with Chinese broccoli and chilli noodles.

Chinese broccoli and chilli noodles: Place noodles in large heatproof bowl, cover with boiling water, stand 3 minutes; drain. Heat wok, add oil then capsicum, garlic and ginger; stir-fry until capsicum is tender. Add broccoli and sauces; cook, stirring, until broccoli is just tender. Add noodles; cook, stirring, until hot.

serves 6

Chinese broccoli (otherwise known as gai lum) is recognisable by its small broccoli-like florets among crisp, dark leaves. Stems and leaves are edible, although thick stems may need to be peeled.

roasted tomatoes with grilled cornbread and walnut gremolata

per serving 2.2g fat; 703kJ

125g	(¾ cup) polenta
110g	(¾ cup) plain flour
3 tsps	baking powder
1 tbsp	raw sugar
1	egg
300ml	buttermilk
8	medium (1.5kg) tomatoes, halved
2 tbsps	balsamic vinegar

walnut gremolata

30g	(¼ cup) walnuts, chopped finely
2 tbsps	finely grated lemon rind
1	clove garlic, crushed
1 cup	finely chopped fresh parsley

Grease deep 18cm-round cake pan; line base with baking paper, grease paper.

Combine polenta, flour, baking powder and sugar in bowl. Stir in combined egg and buttermilk; stir until just combined. Pour cornbread mixture into prepared pan. Place tomatoes cut side up on lightly oiled oven tray; drizzle with vinegar. Bake bread and tomatoes in moderate oven (180°C) about 25 minutes or until bread is cooked when tested and tomatoes are lightly browned and softened. Serve cornbread warm or cold with tomatoes and walnut gremolata.

Walnut gremolata: Combine all ingredients in small bowl; mix well.

NB: You can grill bread slices on oiled grill pan or on the barbecue.

serves 8

saffron cinnamon couscous

per serving 3.2g fat; 1506kJ

875ml	(3½ cups) chicken stock
1 tsp	saffron threads, crushed
4	cinnamon sticks
600g	(3 cups) couscous
2 tsps	vegetable oil
2	medium (340g) Spanish onions, chopped
3	cloves garlic, crushed
2	birdseye chillies, seeded, chopped
2 tsps	ground cumin

Combine stock, saffron and cinnamon sticks in small pan. Simmer, covered, 15 minutes; remove cinnamon sticks. Combine couscous and hot stock in large bowl, stand 5 minutes or until stock is absorbed. Fluff couscous with fork. Heat oil in large pan, cook onion, garlic, chillies and cumin, stirring, until onion is soft. Add couscous to pan, stir until heated through.

serves 6

chinese spinach polenta wedges

per serving 10.6g fat; 718kJ

30g	butter
6	green onions, finely chopped
125g	Chinese spinach, chopped
2	cloves garlic, crushed
50g	(⅓ cup) plain flour
2 tbsps	polenta
250ml	(1 cup) milk
4	eggs, separated
20g	(¼ cup) coarsely grated parmesan cheese

Oil 19cm x 29cm rectangular slice pan. Line with baking paper, extending paper 2cm over edge of long sides of pan. Heat butter in medium pan, cook onions, spinach and garlic, stirring, until soft. Stir in flour and polenta, stir over heat 1 minute. Remove from heat, gradually stir in milk. Return to heat, cook, stirring, until mixture boils and thickens. Remove from heat, stir in lightly beaten egg yolks and parmesan. Transfer mixture to large bowl. Beat egg whites in small bowl with electric mixer until soft peaks form, fold into polenta mixture in 2 batches. Spread mixture into prepared pan; bake in hot oven about 12 minutes or until browned. Turn onto board, cut into wedges. Serve immediately.

serves 6

roasted tomatoes with grilled cornbread and walnut gremolata

saffron cinnamon couscous

chinese spinach polenta wedges

roast pork and apples
with mustard fruits

per serving 14.4g fat; 2456kJ

8	small (1kg) apples
500ml	(2 cups) apple juice
160ml	(2/3 cup) apple cider vinegar
1.25kg	boneless rolled pork loin
	Cooking oil spray
2 tsps	cornflour

mustard fruits

220g	(1 cup) caster sugar
250ml	(1 cup) water
2	cinnamon sticks
300g	(2 cups) dried apricots
9	(200g) dried pears
80ml	(1/3 cup) apple cider vinegar
1 tbsp	dry mustard

Slit skin around centre of apples, place apples in baking dish; pour over juice and vinegar. Remove skin and all fat from pork, spray lightly with oil and place on oiled wire rack; put pork and rack on top of apples in dish. Bake, uncovered, in moderate oven (180°C) about 1 hour or until apples are tender. Remove apples from dish, wrap in foil, return pork to dish, bake another 1 hour or until pork is tender. Remove pork from dish, cover with foil to keep warm. Skim away fat from pan juices. Stir in cornflour blended with 2 tsps water and stir until sauce boils. Serve pork immediately with apples, mustard fruits and sauce.

Mustard fruits: Combine 165g (3/4 cup) of the sugar with the water in medium pan, stir over low heat until sugar is dissolved. Add cinnamon and fruit to pan; stir, over low heat, about 10 minutes or until fruit is soft. Add remaining sugar and vinegar to pan, stir about 5 minutes or until thick and syrupy. Cool slightly, stir in mustard.

serves 8

As a result of new and careful production techniques over the past decade, the overall fat content of pork has been reduced by between 60 and 65 per cent.

bok choy with pork filling

per serving 1.6g fat; 214kJ

3	dried shiitake mushrooms
250g	pork and veal mince
½	small (75g) red capsicum, finely chopped
1	small (80g) onion, finely chopped
1	clove garlic, crushed
1 tbsp	mild sweet chilli sauce
2 tsps	oyster sauce
2 tsps	hoisin sauce
2 tsps	soy sauce
8	(1.2kg) baby bok choy

Place mushrooms in heatproof bowl, cover with boiling water, stand 20 minutes; drain. Discard stems; chop caps finely. Combine mushrooms in a bowl with mince, capsicum, onion, garlic and sauces. Divide mixture into 8. Spoon mixture into the centre of each bunch of bok choy, enclose mixture with leaves. Tie bok choy with string. Place in single layer in a steamer over a wok or pan of simmering water; steam, covered, until tender. Serve immediately.

serves 8

A bamboo steamer is an attractive and authentic form of oven-to-tableware. Steamers cost only a few dollars from Asian food markets. Remember to place the steamer on a plate before placing on the table, in order to catch any leakages.

pork steak with mango salsa

per serving 4g fat; 887kJ

4	(500g) lean pork butterfly steaks
1 tbsp	seeded mustard
1 tbsp	grated fresh ginger
2 tsps	olive oil
50g	baby spinach leaves

mango salsa

1	medium (430g) mango
60g	golden shallots, finely sliced
1/3 cup	coriander leaves
80ml	(1/3 cup) raspberry vinegar

Cut butterfly steaks in half. Combine mustard, ginger and oil, spread over steaks. Heat a non-stick frying pan, cook steaks for 2 minutes on each side or until just cooked through. Serve steaks with spinach and mango salsa.

Mango salsa: Peel mango, remove flesh from seed. Cut mango into strips. Combine mango, shallots, coriander and vinegar.

serves 4

steamed pork dumplings
with plum sauce

per serving 1.9g fat; 1087kJ

4	**Chinese dried mushrooms**
250g	**lean minced pork**
1	**green onion, finely chopped**
1	**clove garlic, crushed**
1 tsp	**grated fresh ginger**
50g	**(¾ cup) stale breadcrumbs**
1 tbsp	**light soy sauce**
2 tsps	**hoisin sauce**
1 tbsp	**chopped coriander leaves**
250g	**fresh thin wheat noodles**
125ml	**(½ cup) plum sauce**

Place mushrooms in a bowl, cover with boiling water, stand 20 minutes; drain. Discard stems, chop caps finely. Combine mushrooms, pork, onion, garlic, ginger, breadcrumbs, sauces and coriander in a bowl. Roll level tbsps of mixture into dumplings. Holding about 6 noodles in your hand, wrap them around each pork dumpling, finishing with noodle ends at the base. Place dumplings, in single layer, about 2cm apart, in a bamboo steamer lined with baking paper. Cook, covered, over a wok or a large saucepan of boiling water for 10 minutes or until dumplings are just cooked through. Serve with plum sauce for dipping.

NB: Dumplings can be prepared a day ahead. To serve hot, cook them just before serving. You will have to use noodles of the same length to achieve a neat result.

serves 4 (makes about 16 small dumplings)

chinese barbecued pork
with soft noodles

per serving 12.5g fat; 1696kJ

400g	thick Hokkien noodles
2 tsps	olive oil
2 tbsps	finely grated fresh ginger
3	cloves garlic, crushed
3	birdseye chillies, seeded, chopped
2 tsps	chopped palm sugar
2	medium (400g) red capsicums, seeded, sliced
6	green onions, sliced
200g	Chinese barbecued pork, sliced
80ml	(⅓ cup) ketjap manis
60ml	(¼ cup) oyster sauce
2 tbsps	chicken stock

Rinse noodles under hot water; drain. Transfer to large bowl; separate noodles with a fork. Heat 1 tsp of oil in wok or large pan; stir-fry ginger, garlic, chilli and palm sugar until fragrant. Add capsicum and onion, stir-fry until capsicum is just soft. Remove vegetables from pan. Heat remaining oil in same wok; stir-fry noodles for 2 minutes. Return vegetables to wok with pork, combined sauces and stock; stir-fry until heated through.

serves 4

"If food is poetry, is not poetry also food?"

JOYCE CAROL OATES

pork and bean curry

per serving 8.9g fat; 1865kJ

1 tbsp	peanut oil
500g	pork rump steaks, cut into 3cm pieces
1	large (200g) onion, sliced
125ml	(½ cup) light coconut milk
250g	dried wheat noodles
150g	green beans, sliced diagonally

yellow curry paste

1	small (100g) Spanish onion, roughly chopped
1 tbsp	roughly chopped fresh lemon grass
4	cloves garlic, coarsely chopped
3	small fresh red chillies, seeded, coarsely chopped
1 tbsp	roughly chopped fresh turmeric
1 tbsp	roughly chopped fresh ginger
2 tsps	coriander seeds
3	fresh coriander roots, coarsely chopped
2 tbsps	fish sauce
3	kaffir lime leaves, torn
2 tsps	sugar

Heat oil in large pan; cook pork, in batches, until browned. Remove and cover to keep warm. Cook onion in same pan, stirring, until onion is soft. Add yellow curry paste; cook, stirring, until fragrant. Return pork to pan with milk; simmer, uncovered, 30 minutes.

Meanwhile, cook noodles in large pan of boiling water, uncovered, until just tender; drain.

Add beans to pork curry in pan; cook, uncovered, until beans are just tender. Gently stir in noodles until just heated through.

Yellow curry paste: Blend or process all ingredients until pureed.

serves 4

red pork fillet
with couscous

per serving 9.2g fat; 1492kJ

60ml	(¼ cup) red curry paste
500g	whole piece pork fillet
2	medium (300g) onions, finely chopped
500ml	(2 cups) beef stock
300g	(1½ cups) couscous
2	medium (380g) tomatoes, finely chopped
⅓ cup	chopped fresh mint leaves
2 tbsps	slivered almonds, toasted

Rub 1 tbsp of the curry paste over pork. Cook pork in large, heated, oiled, non-stick pan, uncovered, until browned all over and cooked as desired. Remove from pan; cover to keep warm.

Cook remaining paste and onion in same pan, stirring, until onion is soft. Add stock, bring to boil; remove from heat. Stir in couscous; stand, covered, 5 minutes. Using fork, gently stir tomato, mint and half the almonds into couscous mixture. Slice pork; serve with couscous sprinkled with remaining almonds.

serves 4

spiced pork skewers with honey glaze

per serving 4.9g fat; 979kJ

500g	pork fillets
2	cloves garlic, crushed
2 tsps	cumin seeds
½ tsp	ground coriander
¼ tsp	ground paprika
2 tsps	olive oil

honey glaze

125ml	(½ cup) orange juice
2 tbsps	honey
2 tbsps	barbecue sauce
2 tbsps	creamy mustard

Cut pork into 3cm cubes, combine with garlic, cumin, coriander, paprika and oil. Thread pork onto skewers. Cook skewers, in batches, in an oiled, heated grill pan 5 minutes or until browned and cooked through, turning occasionally. Serve with honey glaze.

Honey glaze: Combine all ingredients in a small saucepan, stir over heat until boiling, reduce heat to low, simmer for 5 minutes or until thickened.

NB: Soak bamboo skewers in water for at least 1 hour before threading the meat onto them to prevent the skewers burning.

serves 4

pork cutlets with caramelised grapefruit

per serving 6.7g fat; 2234kJ

1kg	butternut pumpkin
10g	lemon thyme
2	large (1kg) ruby red grapefruit
1	large (300g) orange
220g	(1 cup) raw sugar
80ml	(⅓ cup) red wine
4	pork cutlets, trimmed

Remove seeds from pumpkin; cut pumpkin into 8 wedges.

Place pumpkin and thyme in large, lightly oiled baking dish; bake in hot oven (220°C) about 20 minutes or until pumpkin is just cooked through and browned. Keep warm.

Meanwhile, remove skin and pith from grapefruit and orange; cut into wedges.

Place sugar in large, heavy-based saucepan; stir over low heat about 5 minutes or until sugar is dissolved. Bring to boil, simmer, uncovered, until sugar changes colour and becomes caramel.

Stir in wine, grapefruit and orange, simmer, uncovered, about 2 minutes or until grapefruit and orange are just darkened in colour and syrup is thick. (If you cook the fruit too much, it will fall apart.)

Cook pork, in batches, in oiled pan until browned on both sides and cooked as desired. Serve pork with pumpkin mixture and caramelised grapefruit and oranges.

serves 4

roast pork with lemon and olives

per serving 7.7g fat; 844kJ

1 tbsp	olive oil
400g	pork fillet
3	slices lemon
350g	pickling onions, peeled
2	cloves garlic, crushed
500ml	(2 cups) chicken stock
1 tbsp	lemon thyme leaves
60g	green olives

Preheat oven to moderately hot (200°C). Heat oil in a baking dish, cook pork over high heat for 2 minutes on each side or until browned; remove. Cook lemon for 2 minutes on each side or until browned; remove. Cook onions and garlic for 3 minutes or until browned. Add lemon, stock and thyme.

Remove from heat, transfer to oven, bake for 15 minutes. Add pork and olives to baking dish, cook for 10 minutes (for medium pork) or until cooked as desired.

Hint: To peel the onions easily, place them in a bowl, cover with boiling water, stand 5 minutes, drain, peel.

serves 4

potato and corn mash

per serving 0.5g fat; 827kJ

5	medium (1kg) desiree potatoes
130g	can corn kernels, drained
1/2	(125ml) cup skim milk

Boil or steam peeled and chopped potatoes until tender, drain, mash. Stir in corn and milk.

serves 4

ginger mashed parsnips

per serving 1.1g fat; 587kJ

500g	parsnips
1	clove garlic, crushed
1 tsp	grated fresh ginger
250ml	(1 cup) chicken or vegetable stock

Peel parsnips, cut into chunks. Combine parsnips, garlic, ginger and stock in a medium pan. Cover, bring to boil, cook over medium heat for 10 minutes or until soft and all liquid has evaporated; remove, mash. (Note: The stock used to cook the parsnip has to be evaporated or the mash will be too wet. Take the lid off at the end of the cooking, if needed. If the stock has evaporated but the parsnip is not yet tender, add a little water.)

NB: Parsnip mash can be used in the same way as mashed potato.

serves 2

fresh pea mash

per serving 0.5g fat; 344kJ

1	small (80g) onion, finely chopped
450g	(3 cups) shelled fresh peas (ie, approx 1.2kg unshelled)
60ml	(1/4 cup) chicken stock

Cook onion, stirring, in heated, oiled pan until soft. Stir in peas; cook, stirring, for 2 minutes. Add stock and bring to boil; simmer, covered, stirring occasionally, for about 10 minutes or until peas are tender. Blend or process pea mixture until almost smooth.

serves 4

celeriac puree

per serving 5.2g fat; 561kJ

2	cloves garlic, unpeeled
1	celeriac (1.25kg)
2 tbsps	skim milk
1 tbsp	extra virgin olive oil
	Salt and pepper, to taste

Bring a medium saucepan of water to boil. Add garlic cloves to water, cook for 3 minutes or until the garlic inside feels very soft, remove, set aside. Peel celeriac, cut into 5cm chunks. Add to boiling water, cook for 10 minutes or until soft. Drain, place into a large bowl. Squeeze the garlic cloves out of their skin into the celeriac. Add milk, oil, salt and pepper, mash until smooth.

NB: Celeriac begins to brown as soon as it comes into contact with the air, so it is important to have the boiling water ready; add the celeriac to the water as you are cutting it.

serves 4

potato and corn mash

fresh pea mash

ginger mashed parsnips

celeriac puree

poultry

baked chicken with french tarragon

per serving 4.3g fat; 865kJ

2 tbsps	low-fat plain yogurt
2 tbsps	Dijon mustard
2 tbsps	lemon juice
4	(680g) chicken breast fillets
	Salt and black pepper
½ cup	chopped fresh tarragon leaves

Preheat oven to moderate (190°C). Cut 4 pieces of aluminium foil large enough to enclose chicken. Combine yogurt, mustard and lemon juice in a bowl, add chicken, toss until coated. Place chicken on foil, sprinkle with salt and pepper, top with tarragon. Bring the sides of the foil up around the chicken, press edges together to seal. Place in a baking dish, bake for 20 minutes or until chicken is just cooked through; serve with juices.

serves 4

Delicious served with rice (to soak up the cooking juices) and a salad or vegetables.

braised spatchcock
with choy sum and potatoes

per serving 6.6g fat, 1149kJ (skin off); 19g fat, 1559kJ (skin on)

2	**500g spatchcocks**
2 tsps	**grated lime rind**
60ml	**(¼ cup) lime juice**
2 tsps	**sweet chilli sauce**
3	**cloves garlic, crushed**
12	**small (480g) new potatoes, unpeeled**
600g	**choy sum, chopped**
2 tbsps	**lime juice, extra**
1 tbsp	**finely chopped fresh coriander leaves**

Cut along both sides of spatchcock backbones; discard backbones. Cut along breast bones, dividing spatchcocks in half. Place spatchcock in large pan of boiling water, simmer, uncovered, about 10 minutes or until just cooked. Remove spatchcock from pan; place, in single layer, in shallow dish. Discard cooking liquid.

Meanwhile, combine rind, juice, sauce and garlic in small jug, pour over spatchcock. Cook spatchcock in large, heated, oiled pan until browned all over and cooked through. Cover to keep warm. Meanwhile, boil, steam or microwave potatoes until just tender; drain and slice thickly. Heat a lightly oiled medium pan; cook potato until golden brown on both sides. Add choy sum; cook, stirring, until just wilted. Serve spatchcock with potato and choy sum mixture; drizzle with extra juice and coriander.

serves 4

"Too much of a good thing can be wonderful."

MAE WEST

spiced roast chicken with corn seasoning

per serving 12.6g fat; 1263kJ

1.5kg	chicken
2 tsps	ground cumin
2 tsps	ground coriander
1 tsp	Mexican-style chilli powder

corn seasoning

1	medium (150g) onion, finely chopped
2	cloves garlic, crushed
310g	can corn kernels, drained
70g	(1 cup) stale breadcrumbs
2 tbsps	chopped fresh coriander leaves
2 tsps	grated lime rind
2 tbsps	lime juice

Rinse chicken under cold water, pat dry inside and out. Fill both cavities with corn seasoning, secure openings with toothpicks. Tie legs of chicken together, tuck wings under. Place chicken on wire rack in baking dish.

Combine spices and spread mixture over chicken. Loosely cover chicken with lightly oiled foil; bake in moderate oven 1¼ hours. Remove foil, bake a further 30 minutes or until chicken is well browned and tender. Serve immediately.

Corn seasoning: Heat lightly oiled pan, cook onion and garlic, stirring, until onion is soft. Combine onion mixture with remaining ingredients in medium bowl.

serves 6

tandoori chicken
with spiced pumpkin and tahini yogurt

per serving 12.8g fat; 1683kJ

1 tsp	cayenne pepper
1 tbsp	ground cumin
1 tbsp	ground coriander
1 tbsp	ground turmeric
2 tsps	sweet paprika
2 tsps	garlic salt
6	(1kg) skinless chicken breast fillets
	Baby rocket leaves, to serve

spiced pumpkin

1	medium (1.6kg) butternut pumpkin, peeled
1 tbsp	grated fresh ginger
1 tsp	ground nutmeg
	Cooking oil spray

tahini yogurt

1 tbsp	tahini
400g	low-fat plain yogurt

Preheat oven to moderately hot (200°C). Combine spices and salt in bowl. Rub spice mixture over chicken breasts, cover; refrigerate 3 hours or overnight. Heat lightly oiled flameproof baking dish over hotplate, add chicken, cook over medium heat for 1 minute on each side or until lightly browned. Transfer to oven, bake for about 10 minutes or until just cooked through. Stand chicken 10 minutes before slicing. Serve with spiced pumpkin, rocket and tahini yogurt.

Spiced pumpkin: Cut pumpkin into wedges, combine with ginger and nutmeg, lightly spray with cooking oil spray. Bake about 20 minutes or until tender.

Tahini yogurt: Combine ingredients in a bowl.

serves 6

chicken breast
with potato wedges and lemon garlic beans

per serving 4.5g fat; 1340kJ

2	medium (400g) potatoes
1	small (250g) kumara
1	egg white, lightly beaten
1/4 tsp	chilli powder
1/4 tsp	ground black pepper
15g	(1/4 cup) dry-packed sun-dried tomatoes
1 tbsp	chopped fresh rosemary
4	(680g) skinless chicken breast fillets

lemon garlic beans

200g	baby green beans
1 tbsp	lemon juice
2	cloves garlic, crushed

Cut each unpeeled potato into 6 wedges; cut peeled kumara into 2cm slices, cut slices in half. Place potato and kumara on a baking-paper-lined baking tray, brush all over with combined egg white, chilli and pepper. Place wedges skin side down, bake in moderately hot oven (200°C) for 30 minutes.

Meanwhile, place sun-dried tomatoes in heatproof bowl, cover with boiling water, stand 5 minutes; drain. Chop tomatoes finely; stir in rosemary. Spread tomato mixture over chicken breasts. Place chicken on wire rack in a baking dish; bake, uncovered, with potatoes and kumara, in moderately hot oven about 15 minutes or until chicken is tender and potatoes are browned. Potatoes will have a total cooking time of about 45 minutes. Serve chicken immediately with potatoes, kumara and lemon garlic beans.

Lemon garlic beans: Boil, steam or microwave beans until tender; drain. Return beans to pan or dish, add juice and garlic, stir until heated through.

serves 4

Kumara is the name given by New Zealand Maoris to the orange variety of sweet potato. Fat-free and rich in vitamin C, the orange-fleshed sweet potatoes have more sugar and dietary fibre than the white-fleshed ones, which are higher in starch. Choose firm, smooth, well-shaped tubers and store in a cool, dark place for up to two weeks – but don't refrigerate.

light 'n' spicy
crumbed chicken

per serving 10.3g fat; 1645kJ

12	**(900g) chicken tenderloins**
50g	**(⅓ cup) plain flour**
2	**egg whites, lightly beaten**
35g	**(⅓ cup) packaged breadcrumbs**
35g	**(⅓ cup) Corn Flake crumbs**
2 tsps	**garlic salt**
1 tsp	**lemon pepper**

Toss chicken in flour; shake away excess flour. Coat chicken in egg, then in combined breadcrumbs, crumbs, salt and pepper. Cover, refrigerate 15 minutes. Place chicken in single layer on oven tray; bake, uncovered, in hot oven (220°C) about 15 minutes or until cooked through.

serves 4

vietnamese rice paper rolls

per serving 8.9g fat; 1957kJ

80g	bean thread noodles
600g	skinless chicken breast fillets
1 tsp	sesame oil
160ml	(²/3 cup) mirin
2 tbsps	chopped fresh lemon grass
80ml	(1/3 cup) ketjap manis
1 tbsp	chopped fresh ginger
2	cloves garlic, crushed
1/2 cup	shredded fresh mint leaves
1	small (100g) Spanish onion, thinly sliced
35g	(1/4 cup) cashews, toasted, chopped
80g	bean sprouts
2	birdseye chillies, seeded, chopped
16	22cm-round rice paper sheets
16	fresh mint leaves, extra
80ml	(1/3 cup) fresh lime juice

Place noodles in small, heatproof bowl, cover with boiling water, stand until just tender; drain. Roughly chop noodles. Cook chicken in heated, oiled pan until browned all over and just cooked through. Cut chicken into thin slices. Combine sesame oil, half the mirin, lemon grass, half the ketjap manis, ginger, garlic and shredded mint in large bowl; stir in noodles, chicken, onion, cashews, bean sprouts and chilli. Cover and refrigerate for 30 minutes. Place 1 sheet of rice paper in large bowl of warm water until just softened; lift from water carefully, place on board. Place 1 mint leaf in centre of rice paper; top with 1 heaped tbsp of filling. Roll to enclose, folding in ends (roll should be about 8cm long). Repeat with remaining rice paper sheets, mint and filling. Combine remaining mirin, ketjap manis and lime juice in small bowl, serve as a dipping sauce with rice paper rolls.

serves 4 (makes 16)

Made from rice flour, water and salt, rice paper sheets are hard and transparent, and are available in a number of sizes and shapes. Before use, they must be softened with water for a few minutes.

chicken with pumpkin and sweet and spicy tomato sauce

per serving 12g fat; 1311kJ

3	**medium (225g) egg tomatoes**
2 tsps	**olive oil**
1	**small (80g) onion, finely chopped**
1	**clove garlic, crushed**
2 tsps	**yellow mustard seeds**
1 tsp	**garam masala**
½ tsp	**ground cumin**
¼ tsp	**ground turmeric**
¼ tsp	**dried chilli flakes**
1 tbsp	**brown sugar**
4	**(680g) chicken breast fillets**
1 tbsp	**olive oil, extra**
	Ground black pepper
250g	**pumpkin, cut into 2cm cubes**
1 tbsp	**lemon juice**

Preheat oven to moderately hot (200°C). Halve tomatoes lengthways, lay cut side up on a baking tray. Bake for 15 minutes or until very soft. Heat oil in a frying pan, cook onion and garlic over medium heat, stirring, for 2 minutes or until softened. Add mustard seeds, garam masala, cumin, turmeric and chilli flakes, stir over heat 1 minute. Add sugar and tomatoes, cook for 5 minutes or until thick and pulpy, stirring often; cool.

Brush chicken fillets with half the extra oil, sprinkle with pepper. Heat a non-stick frying pan, cook chicken over medium heat for 4 minutes on each side or until just cooked through; remove, cover with foil. Heat remaining oil in pan, cook pumpkin over high heat, stirring, for 5 minutes or until golden brown and tender; stir in lemon juice.

To serve, slice chicken, top with pumpkin, spoon over tomato sauce.

serves 4

coriander chicken with avocado salsa

per serving 12.9g fat; 1226kJ

4	**medium (680g) skinless chicken breast fillets**
1 cup	**chopped fresh coriander leaves**

avocado salsa

½	**small (50g) Spanish onion, finely chopped**
1	**clove garlic, crushed**
1	**birdseye chilli, seeded, finely chopped**
2	**medium (380g) vine-ripened tomatoes, chopped**
2 tbsps	**chopped fresh coriander leaves**
1	**medium (250g) ripe avocado, chopped**
1 tbsp	**fresh lemon juice**

Season chicken fillets with a little sea salt and freshly ground black pepper, cook on oiled barbecue bars until lightly browned all over. Top each chicken fillet with coriander and continue to barbecue until just cooked through. Serve with avocado salsa.

Avocado salsa: Combine all ingredients in a bowl and stir until just combined.

serves 4

"There is no sincerer love than the love of food."
GEORGE BERNARD SHAW

Guest Chef
Gwenael Lesle
Friends

spiced duck breast
with spinach and mushroom salad

per serving 12.9g fat; 1024kJ

4	**(600g) duck breast fillets***
2 tsps	**ground ginger**
1 tsp	**celery salt**
1 tsp	**paprika**
1 tsp	**ground cumin**
1/4 tsp	**ground white pepper**
pinch	**ground mace (or nutmeg)**
2 tsps	**hazelnut oil**
200g	**oyster mushrooms**
125g	**baby spinach leaves**
1	**green onion, chopped**
1 tbsp	**Jerez vinegar****
	Salt and pepper, to taste
1 tbsp	**finely chopped macadamia nuts**

Remove the skin from the duck breasts. Combine ginger, celery salt, paprika, cumin, white pepper and mace, sprinkle over duck breasts.

Heat a non-stick frying pan. Cook duck over medium-low heat for 2 minutes on each side (for rare) or until just cooked through. Remove, set aside. Wipe out pan with absorbent paper. Add hazelnut oil and mushrooms to pan, cook over high heat, stirring, for 1 minute or until softened; remove. Combine mushrooms in a bowl with spinach, onion, vinegar, salt and pepper, toss until combined. Arrange on serving plates, top with sliced duck breasts, sprinkle with macadamia nuts.

* You could use chicken breast fillets instead of duck, if preferred.
** Jerez is a Spanish sherry vinegar. If unavailable, a good red wine vinegar can be used instead.

serves 4

chicken, leek and potato pies

per serving 10.5g fat; 1963kJ

1kg	chicken breast fillets, coarsely chopped
2	small (400g) leeks, thickly sliced
750g	potatoes, coarsely chopped
50g	(1/3 cup) plain flour
180ml	(3/4 cup) skim milk
250ml	(1 cup) chicken stock
	Sea salt and pepper, to taste
12	sheets filo pastry
1	egg white, lightly beaten

Cook chicken in batches in large, heated, non-stick saucepan, until browned; remove.

Cook leek and potato in same pan, stirring, until leek is soft. Add flour; cook, stirring, until mixture bubbles. Remove from heat, gradually stir in milk and stock; cook, stirring, until mixture boils and thickens. Season with salt and pepper. Remove from heat; stir in chicken. Spoon filling into 6 x 250ml (1-cup) ovenproof dishes.

Top each dish with 2 sheets of pastry scrunched up. Brush with egg white. Bake in moderate oven (180°C) about 20 minutes or until pastry is browned.

serves 6

crumbed tenderloin
with light mandarin sauce

per serving 9.6g fat; 1143kJ

125ml	(½ cup) mandarin juice
1 tsp	mandarin zest, finely diced
1 tsp	lemon zest, finely diced
½ tsp	sugar
½ tsp	mild English mustard
1 tsp	cornflour
1 tsp	water
1 tsp	salt
1 tsp	white pepper
70g	(1 cup) packaged breadcrumbs
500g	chicken tenderloins
1	egg, lightly beaten
	Cooking oil spray

Place juice, zests and sugar in small pan and bring to gentle simmer. Combine mustard with blended cornflour and water, then add to sauce, stirring until it thickens. Remove from heat.

Combine salt, pepper and breadcrumbs. Coat each tenderloin with beaten egg then breadcrumb mixture. Spray with oil and bake in hot oven (220°C) for about 15 minutes or until golden.

Drizzle mandarin sauce over chicken to serve.

serves 4

caramelised onion and potato frittata

per serving 4.5g fat; 837kJ

4	large (800g) brown onions, thinly sliced
50g	(1/4 cup) brown sugar
60ml	(1/4 cup) balsamic vinegar
2	large (600g) potatoes
160ml	(2/3 cup) skim milk
3	eggs
4	egg whites
40g	(1/3 cup) reduced-fat grated cheddar cheese
2 tbsps	chopped fresh lemon thyme leaves
50g	mixed lettuce leaves

Oil a 19cm-round cake pan, line base with baking paper, and set aside. Put onions in large, heated, lightly oiled saucepan, cook, stirring, until onion is soft. Stir in sugar and vinegar, cook over low heat for 10 minutes or until golden brown; stir occasionally. Boil, steam or microwave potatoes until tender; drain. Slice potatoes thickly, layer in prepared pan. Top with caramelised onion. Pour combined milk, eggs, egg whites, cheese and thyme over onion. Bake, uncovered, in moderate oven (180°C) for 35 minutes or until frittata is firm. Serve hot or cold with lettuce.

serves 6

saffron scrambled eggs on corn cakes

per serving 4.5g fat; 1108kJ

2	(720g) corn cobs
6	egg whites
225g	(1 1/2 cups) plain flour
2 tsps	sweet paprika
2 tbsps	chopped fresh coriander leaves
125ml	(1/2 cup) skim milk
4	eggs
2	egg whites, extra
pinch	saffron threads

Cut corn kernels from cobs. Beat egg whites in large bowl with electric mixer until soft peaks form. Combine corn, flour, paprika and coriander in large bowl; stir in milk, mix until combined. Fold in egg whites.

Cook 60ml (1/4 cup) of corn mixture in heated, oiled, heavy-based pan until brown on both sides and cooked through. Repeat with remaining mixture.

Combine eggs, extra egg whites and saffron in medium bowl; beat lightly with a fork. Cook egg in lightly oiled non-stick pan, stirring gently, until creamy and firm.

Serve scrambled eggs on corn cakes.

serves 8

egg white omelette with asparagus

per serving 9g fat; 1400kJ

200g	asparagus, chopped
4	bacon rashers
2	green onions, sliced
90g	(3/4 cup) grated reduced-fat cheddar cheese
8	egg whites
300g	unsliced mixed-grain bread

Boil, steam or microwave asparagus until tender; drain, rinse under cold water, drain well.

Remove rind and fat from bacon, chop bacon. Heat a dry, non-stick pan, add bacon and onions, cook, stirring, until bacon is browned. Combine asparagus with bacon mixture and cheese in bowl; cover to keep warm.

Beat egg whites in large bowl with electric mixer until soft peaks form. Spread a quarter of egg whites into a heated, non-stick pan, cook until lightly browned underneath. Place pan under grill until top of omelette is just set. Spoon a quarter of the asparagus mixture over one half of omelette, fold in half; slide onto serving plate. Repeat with remaining egg whites and asparagus mixture to make 4 omelettes. Meanwhile, cut bread into 4 slices; toast bread. Serve omelettes immediately with toast slices.

NB: The omelette pan should be unscratched or should be sprayed lightly with cooking oil spray.

serves 4

caramelised onion and potato frittata

saffron scrambled eggs on corn cakes

egg white omelette with asparagus

seafood

spiced trout with cucumber and yogurt

per serving 12.9g fat; 1476kJ

2	**150g ocean trout fillets**
2 tsps	**olive oil**
	Freshly ground black pepper
1 tsp	**ground cumin**
½ tsp	**ground paprika**
¼ tsp	**ground chilli**
1	**small (100g) Lebanese cucumber**
50g	**baby spinach leaves**
300g	**chat potatoes, steamed**
2 tbsps	**low-fat plain yogurt**
2 tbsps	**chopped fresh mint**

Brush trout with oil, dust with combined pepper, cumin, paprika and chilli. Heat a non-stick frying pan, cook trout over medium-high heat for 1 minute on each side or until just cooked. Finely shred (or coarsely grate) cucumber, drain on absorbent paper. Serve trout on a bed of baby spinach, top with cucumber, thickly sliced potatoes, yogurt and mint.

serves 2

When buying trout fillets, look for firm, moist flesh that is bright, lustrous and pink. To store, wrap fillets individually in plastic wrap or place them in an airtight container. Refrigerate for 2-3 days or freeze for up to 6 months.

roasted baby red mullet
with vietnamese mint

per serving 9.9g fat; 1157kJ

2	(800g) telegraph cucumbers
2 tbsps	finely chopped palm sugar
6	fresh kaffir lime leaves, shredded
⅓ cup	firmly packed fresh Vietnamese mint leaves, shredded
2	birdseye chillies, seeded, chopped
2 tbsps	lime juice
1 tbsp	fish sauce
2 tbsps	thinly sliced lemon grass
3	green onions, thinly sliced
4	160g whole red mullet, cleaned

Along with other oily fish, mullet is rich in omega-3 fatty acids, which are thought to reduce the risk of cardiac arrest, extend life expectancy, lower blood pressure and cholesterol levels, lessen the symptoms of rheumatoid arthritis and even ease depression.

Thinly slice cucumbers, lengthways, using a vegetable peeler. Combine palm sugar, lime leaves, mint, chillies, juice, fish sauce, lemon grass and onions in small bowl. Remove 2 tbsps of mixture, combine with cucumbers. Fill fish with remaining mixture; roast in moderate oven (180°C) 15 minutes or until just cooked through. Serve fish with cucumber mixture.

serves 4

There are about 20 species of garfish in Australian waters. They can be distinguished by the length of their "beaks" and by their colour. Usually sold whole, they can be fried, baked, grilled or poached. The flesh is fine, sweet and delicately flavoured.

spiced garfish
with roasted tomatoes and couscous

per serving 6.2g fat; 1328kJ

4	**medium (760g) tomatoes, halved**
12	**medium (1.5kg) whole garfish**
50g	**(⅓ cup) plain flour**
1 tbsp	**ground cumin**
2 tsps	**olive oil**
	Snow pea tendrils, if desired

couscous

250ml	**(1 cup) boiling water**
200g	**(1 cup) couscous**

Place tomatoes, cut side up, on wire rack in baking dish. Bake tomatoes in very hot oven (240°C) about 20 minutes or until tender.

Meanwhile, toss fish in combined flour and cumin; shake off excess.

Heat oil in large non-stick pan; cook fish, in batches, until browned lightly on both sides. Transfer fish to lightly oiled wire rack in baking dish. Bake in very hot oven 10 minutes or until fish is just cooked through.

Serve fish with tomatoes and couscous. Garnish with snow pea tendrils, if desired.

Couscous: Pour the water over couscous in medium bowl, cover, stand about 5 minutes or until water is absorbed. Fluff with a fork to separate grains.

serves 4

salmon with spice crust

per serving 15.2g fat; 1240kJ

1 tbsp	ground cumin
2 tsps	ground turmeric
1 tbsp	grated fresh ginger
1 tbsp	finely chopped lemon grass
4	kaffir lime leaves, finely chopped (or 2 tsps grated lime rind)
1 tbsp	lime juice
2 tbsps	chopped fresh coriander leaves
4	fresh red chillies, seeded, finely chopped
2 tsps	peanut oil
4	200g thick salmon fillets
350g	snake beans
1	clove garlic, crushed
1 tbsp	soy sauce

Combine spices, ginger, lemon grass, lime leaves, juice, coriander, chillies and half the oil in small bowl. Heat lightly oiled large non-stick pan, cook salmon until browned on both sides. Transfer salmon to oven tray, spread spice mixture over one side of salmon. Bake in moderately hot oven (200°C) about 10 minutes or until salmon is cooked through. Meanwhile, cut beans into 15cm lengths. Heat large pan or wok, add remaining oil, then garlic and beans, stir-fry until just tender. Serve salmon immediately with beans; drizzle with soy sauce.

serves 4

"Food is to eat, not to frame and hang on the wall."
WILLIAM DENTON

grilled atlantic salmon
with green pawpaw salad
and palm sugar vinaigrette

per serving 12.2g fat; 1781kJ

4	**200g skinned Atlantic salmon fillets**
1	**small (650g) green pawpaw, coarsely grated**
1/2	**small (50g) Spanish onion, thinly sliced**
1/2 cup	**fresh Vietnamese mint leaves**
1/3 cup	**fresh Thai basil leaves**

palm sugar vinaigrette

135g	**(1/2 cup) chopped palm sugar**
2	**red Thai chillies, seeded, thinly sliced**
1/2 tsp	**fish sauce**
1	**clove garlic, crushed**
80ml	**(1/3 cup) lime juice**

Cook salmon in oiled grill pan (or grill or barbecue) until lightly browned on both sides and cooked as desired. Combine pawpaw, onion, mint and basil in medium bowl. Serve salmon topped with pawpaw mixture and drizzled with palm sugar vinaigrette.

Palm sugar vinaigrette: Combine sugar, chilli, sauce and garlic in small pan; cook over low heat, stirring, about 5 minutes or until sugar is dissolved and caramelises. Remove from heat; stir in juice.

serves 4

"Our minds are like our stomachs; they are whetted by the change of their food, and variety supplies both with fresh appetites."

QUINTILIAN

red fish curry

per serving 6.4g fat; 1539kJ

6	**birdseye chillies, seeded**
1/2 tsp	**black peppercorns**
1 tbsp	**ground cumin**
1	**small (100g) Spanish onion, chopped**
1 tbsp	**chopped fresh lemon grass**
2	**cloves garlic, peeled**
1/2 tsp	**paprika**
1 tbsp	**fish sauce**
1/4 cup	**chopped fresh coriander leaves**
1	**medium (150g) onion, chopped**
500ml	**(2 cups) vegetable stock**
250g	**fresh or frozen broad beans, peeled**
1kg	**firm white fish fillets, chopped**
125ml	**(1/2 cup) light coconut milk**

If you'd prefer to remove some of the heat from small red chillies, halve the chillies, then seed and thinly slice them. Place slices in ice-cold water and allow to stand for 5 minutes before draining.

Blend or process chillies, peppercorns, cumin, Spanish onion, lemon grass, garlic, paprika, sauce and coriander until almost smooth. In heated non-stick pan, cook onion, stirring, until soft. Add chilli paste; stir until fragrant. Add stock, bring to boil; add broad beans and fish; cook, stirring, about 3 minutes or until fish is just cooked through. Stir in coconut milk; simmer, uncovered, until hot.

serves 6

angel hair with wok-seared prawns
and warm tomato and dill salsa

per serving 4.6g fat; 2117kJ

6	small (780g) vine-ripened tomatoes, quartered
375g	angel hair pasta
16	large uncooked prawns
2 tsps	olive oil
1	clove garlic, crushed
1	small (100g) Spanish onion, finely chopped
2 tbsps	chopped fresh dill
80ml	(⅓ cup) chicken stock

Remove and discard seeds from tomatoes, slice tomatoes. Cook pasta in large pan of boiling, salted water, according to directions on packet; drain. Keep warm. Peel and devein prawns. Heat oil in wok or large pan; cook prawns, in batches, for 2-3 minutes or until pink and just cooked through. Keep warm.

Cook garlic and onion in wok, stirring, until onion is soft. Add tomatoes, dill and stock; cook, stirring, until heated through. Divide pasta between serving bowls, top with tomato mixture and prawns.

serves 4

After cooking pasta, only ever rinse it if it is to be used in a cold dish.
Rinsing removes the starch layer that, in hot dishes, binds the sauce to the pasta.

salmon with slow-roasted fennel and tarragon

per serving 12.9g fat; 1171kJ

6	baby fennel, trimmed, halved
	Sea salt
	Freshly ground black peppercorns
125ml	(½ cup) chicken stock
60ml	(¼ cup) white wine
⅓ cup	fresh tarragon leaves
2 tsps	finely grated lemon rind
6	180g Atlantic salmon fillets

Place fennel in large baking dish; sprinkle with salt and pepper. Add stock, wine, tarragon and rind; bake in slow oven (150°C) about 40 minutes or until fennel is tender.

Cook salmon, in batches, in oiled frying pan until lightly browned on both sides and cooked as desired. Serve salmon with fennel mixture.

serves 6

lobster tails with blood plums

per serving 0.1g fat; 396kJ

4	(1.2kg) uncooked lobster tails
60ml	(¼ cup) fish stock
2 tbsps	chopped fresh oregano leaves
1 tbsp	chopped fresh tarragon leaves
4	stalks fresh lemon grass

6	(500g) blood plums
1	birdseye chilli, seeded, finely chopped
4	kaffir lime leaves, halved
¼ cup	finely chopped palm sugar
2 tbsps	lime juice

Remove lobster tails from shells, combine in large bowl with stock, oregano and tarragon; cover, refrigerate 3 hours or overnight. Cut lemon grass stalks into 15cm lengths, leaving the base intact. Push a lemon grass stalk along the length of each lobster tail. Cook in heated, oiled grill pan (or grill or barbecue), until browned on both sides and just cooked through; brush with remaining marinade during cooking. Serve with palm sugar and blood plum sauce, and with extra grilled plums, if desired.

Palm sugar and blood plum sauce: Halve plums, remove seeds, chop roughly. Combine with remaining ingredients in large pan, bring to boil, simmer, uncovered, for 10 minutes or until plums are very soft; remove lime leaves. Blend or process until smooth.

serves 4

grilled lemon prawns
with corn cakes and rocket salsa

per serving 5.2g fat; 1517kJ

32	large uncooked prawns
2	cloves garlic, crushed
6 tsps	finely grated lemon rind
4 tbsps	chicken stock
4 tsps	freshly ground black pepper

corn cakes

3	medium (1.2kg) kumara
7	trimmed (1.75kg) fresh corn cobs
2	small (160g) brown onions, finely chopped
2	cloves garlic, finely crushcd

rocket salsa

500g	rocket, shredded
4	small (520g) well-ripened tomatoes, chopped
2	small (160g) brown onions, finely chopped
4 tsps	olive oil

Shell and devein prawns, leaving tails intact. Combine prawns, garlic, lemon rind, stock and black pepper in small bowl. Cover and refrigerate for at least 30 minutes.

Drain prawns from marinade, discard marinade. Thread each prawn onto a wooden skewer. Grill for 2 minutes on each side or until just cooked through. Serve with corn cakes and rocket salsa.

Corn cakes: Boil, steam or microwave kumara until tender; drain and mash. Remove kernels from corn cobs. Cook onion and garlic in heated, oiled pan until soft; add corn kernels and cook, stirring, until lightly browned. Combine kumara and corn mixture in a bowl. Shape 2 tbsps of mixture into a small, round cake. Repeat with remaining mixture. Refrigerate for 30 minutes. Cook corn cakes in batches in large, heated, oiled pan until lightly browned all over. Keep warm.

Rocket salsa: Combine all ingredients in small bowl.

serves 8

tartare of salmon
with preserved lemon couscous

per serving 12.8g fat; 1745kJ

750g	salmon fillet (preferably skinless)
2 tbsps	finely chopped chives
1 tsp	ground sea salt
½ tsp	ground black pepper
250ml	(1 cup) chicken stock
2 tsps	raw sugar
200g	(1 cup) instant couscous
¼ cup	finely sliced preserved lemon
1 tbsp	salmon roe

dressing

1 tsp	raw sugar
3 tsps	pink peppercorns, drained
2 tsps	chopped fresh chervil
80ml	(⅓ cup) chicken stock
2 tsps	lime juice

Remove and discard any skin and bones from salmon, dice salmon finely. Combine in small bowl with chives, salt and black pepper. Bring stock and sugar to boil in small pan, add to couscous in medium bowl; cover, stand 5 minutes or until liquid is absorbed. Fluff with fork to separate grains, stir in lemon, cool. Top salmon with roe; drizzle with dressing. Serve with couscous, and a green salad and crusty bread, if desired.

Dressing: Combine all ingredients in jar; shake well.

serves 4

salade niçoise

per serving 7.1g fat; 1260kJ

4	medium (300g) egg tomatoes
8	small (320g) chat potatoes, halved
200g	green beans
2	250g tuna steaks
2	(150g) trimmed celery sticks, thinly sliced
1	medium (170g) Spanish onion, thinly sliced
8	anchovy fillets, drained
8	niçoise olives*, drained
12	baby gherkins, drained
2 tbsps	fresh basil leaves
125ml	(½ cup) chicken stock
60ml	(¼ cup) lemon juice
1	clove garlic, crushed
1 tsp	raw sugar

Cut tomatoes into wedges; remove seeds.

Boil, steam or microwave potatoes until just tender; drain.

Trim beans, then boil, steam or microwave them until just tender; drain.

Cook tuna in heated, oiled grill pan (or grill or barbecue) until browned on both sides and cooked as desired. Cut tuna into large pieces.

Combine tomatoes, potatoes, beans and tuna with celery, onion, anchovies, olives, gherkins and torn basil leaves.

Put stock, lemon juice, garlic and sugar in a jar and shake to combine, then drizzle over salad.

* Niçoise olives are small, oval and brownish-black, with a rich, nutty, mellow flavour. If unavailable, substitute with kalamata olives.

serves 4

tomato swordfish and artichokes
with pastry triangles

per serving 10.4g fat; 1297kJ

½	**slice prepared puff pastry, thawed**
1 tbsp	**olive oil**
1	**medium (170g) Spanish onion, thinly sliced**
2	**cloves garlic, crushed**
4	**medium (760g) tomatoes, peeled, chopped**
1 tbsp	**tomato paste**
250ml	**(1 cup) fish stock (or chicken stock)**
400g	**can artichokes in water, drained, halved**
750g	**swordfish steaks, cut into 3cm cubes**
¼ cup	**chopped fresh flat-leaf parsley**

Preheat oven to moderately hot (200°C). Cut pastry into 4 rectangles, cut each rectangle into 2 triangles. Place triangles on a baking tray lined with baking paper; bake for 10 minutes or until golden brown.

Heat oil in a frying pan, cook onion and garlic over low heat until golden brown. Add tomatoes, tomato paste and stock, cook for 5 minutes or until reduced by half. Add artichokes and fish, cook for 5 minutes or until fish is just cooked through, stirring occasionally. Spoon into serving bowls, sprinkle with parsley. Serve with pastry.

serves 4

thai-style fish and corn cakes

per serving 8.1g fat; 1151kJ

750g	redfish fillets
1 tbsp	grated fresh ginger
1	large fresh red chilli, seeded, chopped
2	cloves garlic, peeled
2	green onions, chopped
1/4 cup	fresh coriander leaves
2 tsps	grated lime rind
1 tbsp	fish sauce
1	egg
1 cup	cooked jasmine rice (equivalent to 65g or 1/3 cup uncooked)
310g	can corn kernels, drained
1 tbsp	peanut oil
1/2	small (400g) fresh pineapple, finely chopped
2 tsps	grated lime rind
1	large fresh red chilli, seeded, finely chopped

Process fish, ginger, chilli, garlic, onions, coriander, rind, sauce and egg until well combined. Transfer fish mixture to large bowl, stir in rice and corn. Roll 2 tbsps mixture into balls, flatten slightly. Heat oil in non-stick pan; cook fish cakes in batches until browned on both sides and cooked through. Serve with pineapple salsa.

Pineapple salsa: Combine all ingredients in bowl; mix well.

serves 6

"I'm fond of anything that comes out of the sea – and that includes sailors."

JANET FLANNER

Guest Chef

Hermann Schneider

Arthurs

skate
with a warm green salad and vinaigrette

per serving 13.4g fat; 1291kJ

4	200g pieces skate*
1 litre	(4 cups) court-bouillon**
1 tbsp	extra virgin olive oil
2 tsps	sherry vinegar
2 tsps	lime juice
2 tbsps	finely chopped red capsicum
1 tbsp	extra virgin olive oil, extra
100g	baby spinach leaves
1	(225g) curly endive (pale centre leaves only)
60g	watercress, trimmed
2	bulbs red witlof, leaves separated
2 tbsps	chopped chervil
1 tbsp	chopped dill
2 tsps	chopped tarragon
	Salt and ground black pepper, to taste

Remove skin from skate. Bring court-bouillon to a slow simmer in a large saucepan. Add skate, cook over low heat for 5 minutes or until just cooked, remove. For the vinaigrette, combine oil, vinegar, lime juice and capsicum in a jar, shake well.

Heat extra oil in a frying pan, toss remaining ingredients over high heat for about 30 seconds or until warmed but still crisp.

Arrange leaves on serving plates, top with skate, drizzle with vinaigrette.

* If skate is unavailable, Hermann suggests using snapper fillets.
** Court-bouillon is a well-flavoured vegetable stock which can be made by boiling water with ingredients such as onion, carrot, leeks and herbs. For this recipe, a ready-prepared vegetable stock can be substituted.

serves 4

yabbies, lemon and pasta

per serving 7.6g fat; 2835kJ

1.8kg	(32) yabbies
2 tsps	olive oil
1	small (80g) onion, finely chopped
2	cloves garlic, crushed
2 tbsps	buttermilk
250ml	(1 cup) fish stock (or vegetable stock)
60ml	(¼ cup) lemon juice
500g	long pasta (eg, fettuccine, tagliatelle)
40g	(¼ cup) caper berries
1 tbsp	shredded lemon rind

Shell and devein yabbies. Heat oil in medium pan; cook onion and garlic, stirring, until onion is soft. Add yabbies, buttermilk, stock and juice to pan; cook, stirring, until yabbies change colour.

Meanwhile, cook pasta in large pan of boiling water, uncovered, until just tender; drain. Gently toss pasta in large bowl with yabbie mixture, caper berries and rind.

serves 4

prawn curry

per serving 6.8g fat; 1035kJ

500g	uncooked king prawns
2 tbsps	tikka masala paste
2 tbsps	mango chutney
80ml	(⅓ cup) vegetable stock
80ml	(⅓ cup) low-fat plain yogurt
½ cup	chopped fresh coriander
1 tbsp	lime juice

Peel and devein prawns. Heat paste and chutney in a non-stick frying pan, add prawns, stir over medium heat until just cooked through. Stir in stock, yogurt, coriander and juice, stir until heated through.

serves 2

trout with
caramelised tomatoes and balsamic

per serving 10.1g fat; 1297kJ

4	**medium (300g) egg tomatoes, quartered lengthways**
2 tsps	**olive oil**
1 tsp	**sugar**
1	**clove garlic, crushed**
	Salt and pepper, to taste
2	**200g ocean trout cutlets**
1 tbsp	**balsamic vinegar**
2 tbsps	**shredded basil leaves**

Combine tomatoes, oil, sugar, garlic, salt and pepper.

Cook trout cutlets in a hot, oiled frying pan for 2 minutes on each side (for rare) or until lightly browned and cooked as desired; remove, set aside. Wipe out pan with absorbent paper.

Cook tomato mixture over high heat in same pan, stirring, for 2 minutes or until softened and lightly browned. Serve fish topped with tomatoes, drizzle with vinegar and sprinkle with basil.

serves 2

spiced blue eye
with sweet tomato relish

per serving 12.4g fat; 1932kJ

4	**(800g) blue eye fillets**
1 tbsp	**grated fresh ginger**
1	**clove garlic, crushed**
2 tsps	**ground turmeric**
2 tsps	**mustard powder**
2 tsps	**sweet paprika**
2 tsps	**dried basil leaves**
2 tsps	**ground fennel**
1/4 tsp	**ground chilli**
1 tsp	**salt**
1 tbsp	**olive oil**

sweet tomato relish

10	**medium (750g) egg tomatoes, halved**
500ml	**(2 cups) water**
250ml	**(1 cup) dry white wine**
1 tbsp	**lime juice**
100g	**(1/2 cup) firmly packed brown sugar**
1 tbsp	**grated lime rind**
1 tbsp	**ground turmeric**
1 tbsp	**yellow mustard seeds**
2	**bay leaves**
2	**stalks lemon grass**

Coat fish with combined remaining ingredients, except oil. Heat oil in a non-stick frying pan, cook fish for 2 minutes on each side or until golden brown and just cooked through.

Serve with sweet tomato relish, and couscous, if desired.

Sweet tomato relish: Combine all ingredients in a medium saucepan. Simmer, uncovered, 30 minutes or until most of the liquid has evaporated. Cool, remove and discard bay leaves and lemon grass.

serves 4

sumac-spiced potato wedges

per serving 0.4g fat; 778kJ

1kg	desiree potatoes
1	egg white, lightly beaten
1 tsp	sumac*
1/4 tsp	ground chilli powder
110g	(1/3 cup) tomato relish**

Preheat oven to very hot (250°C). Cut unpeeled potatoes into wedges. Combine egg white, sumac and chilli in a large bowl. Add potato wedges, combine well. Line a baking tray with baking paper. Place wedges, skin side down, on tray. Bake for 40 minutes or until tender and golden brown. Serve with relish for dipping.

Sumac is a reddish-purple ground spice made from the berries of a shrub grown wild in Lebanon. It is available from some cookshops and delicatessens. If unavailable, use ground paprika.

**Tomato relish is available from delicatessens. Sweet chilli sauce or tomato sauce can be used instead.*

serves 4

herb and yogurt chutney

serve as an accompaniment to rice and curries or with baked or grilled seafood, meats or chicken

per serving 5g fat; 285kJ

80ml	(1/3 cup) low-fat plain yogurt
2 tbsps	finely chopped raw unsalted peanuts
2 tbsps	chopped shredded coconut
2 tbsps	chopped fresh coriander leaves
1 tbsp	chopped fresh mint
2 tsps	grated fresh ginger
2 tsps	lemon juice
pinch	chilli powder
1/2 tsp	sugar

Combine all ingredients in a bowl; refrigerate chutney at least 1 hour before serving.

serves 4

thai coconut sauce

this is a multipurpose sauce, ideal as an accompaniment to grilled or baked meats, chicken, fish and seafood

per serving 2.4g fat; 151kJ

160ml	(2/3 cup) light coconut cream
125ml	(1/2 cup) water
1 tsp	grated lime rind
2 tsps	lime juice
2 tsps	grated fresh ginger
1 tbsp	chopped lemon grass
1 tbsp	chopped fresh mint
4	coriander roots, chopped
2 tbsps	chopped fresh coriander leaves
1 tbsp	sweet chilli sauce
2 tsps	fish sauce

Combine all ingredients in a blender or food processor, blend until finely chopped. Refrigerate sauce for at least 1 hour before serving.

serves 6

strawberry scarlet salsa

this salsa makes an unusual accompaniment for barbecued meat, poultry, seafood, halved avocados or for cheese and greens

per serving 0.1g fat; 51kJ

250g	strawberries, hulled
	Juice of 1 lime or lemon
2 tsps	diced seeded hot chilli
4	spring onions, trimmed, sliced
1/4 tsp	coarsely ground black pepper
1/2 tsp	rock salt
	Fine slivers of lime or lemon zest

Cut strawberries into fine dice or slices, then toss carefully with the remaining ingredients except zest. Set aside for 5-10 minutes, then transfer to a serving bowl and scatter with lime zest.

serves 6

sumac-spiced potato wedges

thai coconut sauce

herb and yogurt chutney

strawberry scarlet salsa

baking

banana bread
with chocolate ricotta

per serving 5g fat; 977kJ

2	small (260g) ripe bananas, mashed
180ml	(3/4 cup) orange juice
300g	(2 cups) self-raising flour
200g	(1 cup) firmly packed brown sugar
1	egg
1	egg white
60g	lite milk chocolate, finely chopped
100g	(1/2 cup) reduced-fat ricotta

Grease a 15cm x 25cm loaf pan. Combine banana and juice in medium bowl; mix well. Add sifted flour and sugar, stir in egg, egg white and 3/4 of the chocolate, pour into prepared pan. Bake in moderate oven (180°C) 1 1/4 hours or until bread is cooked when tested. Cool bread in pan 5 minutes, transfer to wire rack; cool. Slice bread, serve with combined remaining chocolate and ricotta.

serves 6 (makes 18 slices)

When recipes call only for egg whites, leftover yolks can be used to make lemon butter. The organisers of your local fete will love you!

chocolate angel food cake

per serving 0.4g fat; 534kJ

75g	(1/2 cup) plain flour
2 tbsps	cocoa powder
150g	(2/3 cup) caster sugar
8	egg whites
1/2 tsp	vanilla essence
1/2 tsp	cream of tartar
1 tsp	icing sugar mixture

Sift together flour, cocoa and 110g (1/2 cup) of the sugar. Beat egg whites, essence and cream of tartar in large bowl with electric mixer until firm peaks form. Gradually add remaining sugar, beat until dissolved. Gently fold sifted dry ingredients into egg white mixture. Pour mixture into an ungreased 21cm baba pan. Bake in moderate oven (180°C) about 40 minutes or until cake springs back when touched. Invert baba pan immediately onto upturned glass or can, so the cake can cool suspended – cake will not fall out of the pan. Leave undisturbed until cold. Shake pan; turn cake out. Dust with sifted icing sugar.

serves 8

coffee and aniseed biscotti

per serving 0.3g fat; 188kJ

2 tbsps	Pernod liqueur
1 tbsp	espresso coffee granules
200g	(1⅓ cups) plain flour
110g	(½ cup) caster sugar
¼ tsp	baking powder
1	egg white
1	egg
250g	fresh raspberries
1 tbsp	caster sugar
1 tbsp	water
2 tsps	balsamic vinegar
200g	low-fat plain yogurt

Heat Pernod in small pan, stir in espresso granules until dissolved, remove from heat. Sift flour, sugar and baking powder into medium bowl, stir in Pernod mixture, egg white and egg. Turn dough onto floured surface; knead until smooth. Shape into 18cm log; place on lightly greased oven tray. Bake in moderate oven (180°C) about 35 minutes or until just browned and crusty; cool. Using a serrated knife, cut log diagonally into 1.5cm slices, place in single layer on oven trays, bake in moderate oven about 30 minutes or until crisp; cool on wire racks. Combine raspberries, sugar, the water and vinegar in small pan, simmer, stirring, until mixture is slightly thickened. Serve biscotti with raspberry mixture and yogurt.

serves 4 (makes 12)

quick mix fruit cake

per serving 6g fat; 1635kJ

750g	**(4 cups) mixed dried fruit**
100g	**(½ cup) red glacé cherries, quartered**
150g	**(⅔ cup) firmly packed brown sugar**
375ml	**(1½ cups) apple juice**
2	**egg whites, lightly beaten**
60ml	**(¼ cup) canola oil**
80ml	**(⅓ cup) skim milk**
2 tbsps	**brandy**
360g	**(2¼ cups) wholemeal self-raising flour**
1 tsp	**mixed spice**
½ tsp	**ground ginger**
1 tbsp	**brandy, extra**

Line base and sides of deep 19cm-square or 22cm-round cake pan with two thicknesses of brown paper and one layer of baking paper, bringing paper 5cm above edge of pan. Combine fruit, cherries, sugar and juice in bowl; cover, stand overnight. Stir in egg whites, oil, milk, brandy and sifted flour and spices. Spread mixture into prepared pan, decorate with extra cherries, if desired. Bake in slow oven 2-2½ hours. Brush extra brandy over top while still in pan, cover cake with foil; cool.

NB: Can be made 1 month ahead.

serves 12

grapefruit lemon syrup cake

per serving 8.7g fat; 1685kJ

170g	(1 cup) instant polenta
50g	(1/3 cup) plain flour
1½ tsps	baking powder
pinch	salt
80ml	(1/3 cup) reduced-fat plain yogurt
2 tbsps	reduced-fat margarine, melted
1 tbsp	olive oil
2 tbsps	finely grated pink grapefruit rind (we used Ruby Red grapefruit)
2 tbsps	grapefruit juice
2	eggs
2	egg whites
165g	(3/4 cup) caster sugar

lemon syrup

110g	(1/2 cup) caster sugar
60ml	(1/4 cup) water
60ml	(1/4 cup) lemon juice

Grease a deep, 18cm-round pan, line base with paper. Sift polenta, flour, baking powder and salt into large bowl. Combine yogurt, margarine, oil, rind and juice in small bowl; mix well. Beat eggs, egg whites and sugar in small bowl with electric mixer until thick and creamy. Beat in yogurt mixture until smooth. Fold in dry ingredients until just combined (do not over-mix). Pour cake batter into prepared pan and bake in moderate oven (180°C) for 50 minutes or until cake is cooked when tested. Remove cake from oven, turn immediately onto wire rack and turn right side up. Drizzle hot lemon syrup over cake; cool.

Lemon syrup: Combine all ingredients in small pan, simmer, stirring, until sugar dissolves. Continue simmering, uncovered, without stirring, for 3 minutes or until syrup has slightly thickened; transfer to heatproof jug.

NB: Make sure you place the hot cake on a wire rack that's been positioned over an oven tray. That way, when you pour the hot syrup over the cake, the tray will catch the overflow and any excess syrup can be poured back over the cake or served, separately, in a jug.

serves 6

mandarin roulade

per serving 3g fat; 1026kJ

55g	(¼ cup) caster sugar
60ml	(¼ cup) water
2	medium (400g) mandarins, peeled, finely chopped
1 tbsp	orange Curaçao or Grand Marnier
2 tbsps	lemon juice

roulade

3	eggs, separated
110g	(½ cup) caster sugar
110g	(¾ cup) self-raising flour
2 tbsps	hot skim milk
2 tbsps	caster sugar, extra

Combine sugar and water in large pan. Cook, stirring, until sugar is dissolved; add mandarin, Curaçao and lemon juice, simmer 15-20 minutes or until mixture is very thick; cool.

Roulade: Grease a 26cm x 32cm Swiss roll pan, line base and sides with greased paper. Beat egg whites in small bowl with electric mixer until soft peaks form; gradually add sugar, beating until dissolved between additions. Add yolks one at a time, beating well until thick and light. Fold in triple-sifted flour and milk. Pour mixture into prepared pan, bake in moderately hot oven (200°C) about 8 minutes or until cooked when tested. Meanwhile, place a sheet of paper the same size as roulade on bench, sprinkle lightly with extra caster sugar. When roulade is cooked, turn immediately onto paper, quickly peel away lining paper. Cut off crisp edge from long sides, spread roulade evenly with mandarin mixture, commence rolling from short side with help of paper. Lift roulade onto a wire rack to cool.

serves 6

"The only way to get rid of a temptation is to yield to it."

OSCAR WILDE

apple buttermilk crumble cake

per serving 7.2g fat; 816kJ

40g	butter
35g	reduced-fat margarine
75g	(1/3 cup) firmly packed brown sugar
1	egg
1	large (200g) apple
150g	(1 cup) self-raising flour
60ml	(1/4 cup) buttermilk
30g	(1/3 cup) rolled oats
1 tbsp	brown sugar, extra
1/4 tsp	ground cinnamon

Grease a deep, 18cm-round cake pan, line base with baking paper. Beat butter, margarine and sugar in small bowl with electric mixer until light and fluffy. Add egg, beat until just combined. Halve, peel and core apple, chop into small pieces. Stir in apple, flour and buttermilk, in 2 batches.

Spread mixture into prepared pan, sprinkle with combined oats, extra brown sugar and cinnamon. Bake in moderate oven (180°C) for 45 minutes or until cake is cooked when tested. Remove cake from oven and cool on wire rack.

serves 8

Choose apples with a firm, smooth skin and store them in the refrigerator to keep the crispness for up to a month.

chocolate cream cheese brownies

per brownie 4.4g fat; 672kJ

100g	dark chocolate, chopped
200g	low-fat cream cheese
440g	(2 cups) caster sugar
2	eggs
2	egg whites
2 tsps	vanilla essence
40g	(1/4 cup) chopped blanched almonds
185g	(1 1/4 cups) plain flour
70g	(2/3 cup) cocoa

Preheat oven to moderate (180°C). Combine chocolate and cream cheese in a heatproof bowl. Place over a saucepan of boiling water until chocolate has melted (or microwave on HIGH for about 1 1/2 minutes). Remove from heat, add sugar, eggs, egg whites and vanilla. Whisk until combined. Add almonds and sifted flour and cocoa, stir until combined. Spread into a greased and lined 28cm x 18cm lamington tin, bake for 40 minutes or until firm. Allow to cool in tin before cutting into squares.

NB: Brownies can be served as they are, dusted with sifted cocoa or, for a treat, drizzled with 60g melted chocolate.

makes 24

peach and almond free-form pie

per serving 7.2g fat; 747kJ

2	**sheets prepared shortcrust pastry**
60g	**(½ cup) ground almonds**
12	**medium (1.8kg) peaches**
2 tbsps	**plain flour**
2 tsps	**ground cinnamon**
	Milk for brushing
2 tbsps	**demerara sugar**

Preheat oven to moderate (180°C). Lay a sheet of baking paper over a 30cm pizza pan*. Lay pastry sheets on top of each other on a floured surface, roll out to a 36cm circle, trim edges if needed. Lay over pizza pan (there will be a 6cm overhang). Sprinkle pastry with ground almonds.

Wash peaches, remove flesh from seeds, slice thickly. Combine peaches with flour and cinnamon. Pile peaches on pastry (not on the overhang). Fold the pastry overhang roughly over the peaches to partially enclose them. Brush pastry with milk, sprinkle all over with sugar. Bake for 45 minutes or until peaches are softened and pastry is crisp and golden brown. Serve warm, straight from the oven, or serve cold.

If you don't have a pizza pan, place the pastry on a large flat baking tray, lined with baking paper.

serves 8

raspberry
poppy seed cake

per serving 7.4g fat; 913kJ

40g	butter
25g	reduced-fat margarine
110g	(½ cup) caster sugar
1	egg
110g	(¾ cup) self-raising flour, sifted
2 tbsps	plain flour, sifted
2 tbsps	poppy seeds
2 tbsps	skim milk
135g	(1 cup) fresh raspberries

raspberry sugar syrup

35g	(¼ cup) fresh raspberries
55g	(¼ cup) caster sugar
60ml	(¼ cup) water

Grease a deep, 18cm-round cake pan, line base with baking paper. Beat butter, margarine and sugar with electric mixer until light and fluffy, add egg, beat well. Stir in both flours, poppy seeds and milk, mix well. Pour mixture into prepared pan, scatter raspberries over the top of the cake. Bake in moderate oven (180°C) for 1 hour or until cooked when tested. Serve cake drizzled with raspberry sugar syrup.

Raspberry sugar syrup: Blend or process raspberries until almost smooth, pass through a small sieve to remove seeds. Combine raspberry puree, sugar and the water in small pan. Simmer, stirring, without boiling, until sugar is dissolved. Boil gently for 3 minutes or until syrup is slightly thickened.

serves 8

Select berries that are plump and brightly coloured. All berries are an excellent source of vitamin C, with half a punnet containing up to a day's supply, and are full of disease-fighting antioxidants, while the seeds are a good source of dietary fibre.

chocolate cake with raspberry ricotta

per serving 4.2g fat; 870kJ

3	eggs
1 tsp	vanilla essence
150g	(²/₃ cup) caster sugar
75g	(½ cup) self-raising flour
25g	(¼ cup) cocoa
2 tbsps	cornflour
1 tbsp	honey
1 tbsp	boiling water
150g	low-fat ricotta cheese
125g	raspberries
2 tbsps	caster sugar, extra

Preheat oven to moderate (180°C). Grease a deep 20cm-round cake pan, line base with baking paper.

Beat eggs and vanilla in a small bowl with an electric mixer until thick and creamy. Add sugar a spoonful at a time, beating until dissolved between additions. Transfer to a large bowl, fold in sifted flour, cocoa and cornflour. Combine honey and the water, fold into mixture. Pour into prepared pan, bake for 35 minutes or until firm in the centre. Turn onto wire rack to cool.

Serve with combined ricotta, raspberries and extra sugar.

serves 8

"If the people have no bread, let them eat cake."

MARIE ANTOINETTE

shortbread triangles

per biscuit 2.9g fat; 278kJ

75g	(⅓ cup) caster sugar
80g	reduced-fat margarine
1 tbsp	water
75g	(½ cup) plain flour
75g	(½ cup) self-raising flour
35g	(¼ cup) rice flour
	Icing sugar, optional

Preheat oven to moderate (180°C). Line 2 baking trays with baking paper.

Combine all ingredients (except icing sugar) in a food processor, beat for a few seconds until almost blended. Turn mixture onto a lightly floured surface, knead until smooth. Roll out to a rectangle 15cm wide and 25cm long. Cut lengthways into 3 strips, cut each strip into 8 triangles. Place onto baking trays, bake for 15 minutes or until lightly browned. Dust with icing sugar, if desired.

makes 24

strawberry hazelnut cake

per serving 7.6g fat; 655kJ

4	**eggs**
55g	**(¼ cup) caster sugar**
50g	**(⅓ cup) self-raising flour**
35g	**(⅓ cup) ground hazelnuts**
200g	**low-fat ricotta cheese**
1 tbsp	**sugar-free strawberry jam**
125g	**strawberries**
	Icing sugar, for dusting

Preheat oven to moderate (180°C). Grease a deep 20cm-round cake tin, line base with baking paper.

Beat eggs and sugar in a small bowl with an electric mixer until thick and creamy. Fold in sifted flour and hazelnuts. Pour into prepared tin, bake for 30 minutes or until golden brown and firm in the centre. Turn onto wire rack to cool.

Combine ricotta, jam and strawberries in a food processor or blender, blend until smooth. Cut cake into 2 layers, fill with ricotta mixture. Dust top with icing sugar.

serves 8

maple pecan cinnamon cookies

per cookie 3g fat; 474kJ

60g	reduced-fat margarine
90g	(1/3 cup) maple syrup
90g	(1/3 cup) golden syrup
1 tsp	bicarbonate of soda
1 tbsp	boiling water
210g	(2 1/3 cups) rolled oats
225g	(1 1/2 cups) plain flour
pinch	salt
150g	(2/3 cup) firmly packed brown sugar
1 tsp	ground cinnamon
30	pecan halves
2 tbsps	maple syrup, extra

Melt margarine, maple and golden syrup in small pan. Combine soda with the water in small jug. Stir into margarine mixture, until well combined.

Combine oats, flour, salt, sugar and cinnamon in large bowl; stir in margarine mixture. Refrigerate, covered, 20 minutes. Roll tablespoons of mixture into balls. Place on lightly greased oven trays 3cm apart. Place a pecan half on top of each ball, flatten slightly. Bake in moderate oven (180°C) about 20 minutes or until lightly browned. Cool on wire rack. Brush hot cookies with extra maple syrup.

makes 30

bramley apple tart with lemon yogurt

per serving 7.5g fat; 1017kJ

110g	(¾ cup) plain flour
2 tbsps	sugar
25g	butter
35g	reduced-fat margarine
1	egg yolk

bramley apple filling

600g	Bramley or green apples, peeled, cored, coarsely chopped
55g	(¼ cup) caster sugar
2 tbsps	lemon juice

lemon yogurt

200g	low-fat plain yogurt
2 tsps	finely grated lemon rind
1 tsp	sugar

Lightly grease 2 x 20cm loose-based flan tins.

Sift flour and sugar into small bowl; rub in butter and margarine until mixture resembles fine breadcrumbs. Stir in yolk; combine until mixture comes together. Wrap in plastic wrap and refrigerate 30 minutes.

Cut dough in half, roll each half out to fit 1 flan tin; gently ease pastry into both tins. Bake blind.*

Spread Bramley apple filling into tart cases; serve with lemon yogurt.

Bramley apple filling: Combine all ingredients in small pan; cook over low heat, covered, stirring occasionally, until apples are very soft. Push through a fine sieve over small bowl.

Lemon yogurt: Combine all ingredients in small bowl; mix well.

* Baking blind: cut out a circle of baking paper about 5cm larger all around than flan tin. Cover pastry with paper, fill with dried beans or rice, place on oven tray. Bake in moderate oven (180°C) for 10 minutes; remove paper and beans carefully from pastry, bake further 10-15 minutes or until pastry is brown and crisp.

serves 6

ginger cake with poached pears

per serving 4.6g fat; 1311kJ

5	**small (900g) ripe Beurre Bosc pears**
125ml	**(½ cup) red wine**
125ml	**(½ cup) water**
80g	**low-fat margarine**
150g	**(⅔ cup) sugar**
2	**eggs, lightly beaten**
125ml	**(½ cup) low-fat milk**
225g	**(1½ cups) self-raising flour**
2 tsps	**ground ginger**
220g	**(1 cup) sugar, extra**

Grease an 18cm-round cake pan; line base with baking paper.

Peel pears and combine with wine and the water in medium saucepan; simmer, uncovered, about 15 minutes or until pears are tender and a deep red colour. Remove pears from wine mixture; cool pears; reserve wine mixture.

Beat margarine, sugar and eggs in large bowl with electric mixer until thick and pale. Stir in milk, flour and ginger; pour into prepared pan. Bake, uncovered, in moderate oven (180°C) about 40 minutes. Turn cake onto wire rack to cool.

Add extra sugar to wine mixture; simmer, uncovered, 15 minutes or until syrup is very thick. Cut a 15cm circle on top of cake (leaving a 3cm border). Cut about ⅓ of the way through the cake; remove centre piece of cake*. Place pears in centre of cake and drizzle with syrup.

You can blend or process the centre piece until it resembles fine breadcrumbs. Toss the crumbs with some cinnamon and bake in a moderate oven until lightly browned. Sprinkle over pears.

serves 10

double chocolate muffins

per muffin 2.4g fat; 696kJ

90g	pitted prunes
125ml	(1/2 cup) warm water
150g	(2/3 cup) caster sugar
180ml	(3/4 cup) skim milk
1	egg
1	egg white
225g	(1 1/2 cups) self-raising flour
25g	(1/4 cup) cocoa
60g	(1/3 cup) Choc Bits

Spray an 80ml (1/3-cup) muffin pan with cooking oil spray or line with paper muffin cases. Combine prunes and the water in a blender, blend until smooth. Add sugar, blend until smooth. Add milk, egg and egg white, beat until just combined. Pour into a bowl. Fold in sifted flour and cocoa, then fold in Choc Bits. Spoon mixture into muffin cases, bake in moderate oven (180°C) for 20 minutes or until firm to touch. Turn onto wire rack to cool.

makes 12

plum and polenta muffins

per muffin 1.4g fat; 1093kJ

825g	can plums in lite syrup
500ml	(2 cups) skim milk
125ml	(1/2 cup) golden syrup
300g	(2 cups) self-raising flour
110g	(2/3 cup) polenta
150g	(2/3 cup) raw sugar
2	eggs, lightly beaten

Preheat oven to moderate (180°C). Line 2 x 3/4-cup, 6-hole muffin tins with paper muffin cases. Spray paper cases with non-stick baking spray.

Drain plums well, remove seeds. Cut plums into 1.5cm chunks, drain on absorbent paper. Heat milk and golden syrup in a small saucepan until syrup liquifies, cool. Sift flour into a bowl, stir in polenta and sugar. Add milk mixture and eggs, whisk until combined. Stir in plums. Spoon into paper cases. Bake for 30 minutes or until golden brown and firm in the centre.

NB: It is important to spray the paper cases with non-stick baking spray as the muffins' low fat content makes the mixture sticky.

makes 12

pear muffins with golden caramel

per muffin 11.9g fat; 1544kJ

2	small (360g) Beurre Bosc pears
300g	(2 cups) self-raising flour
220g	(1 cup) caster sugar
2	eggs
125g	unsalted butter, melted
160ml	(2/3 cup) reduced-fat milk
4	dried pear halves, chopped
30g	pecans, roughly chopped

golden caramel

220g	(1 cup) caster sugar
250ml	(1 cup) water

Heat oven to moderately hot (200°C). Peel, core and quarter pears. Chop up 6 of the quarters. Thinly slice remaining 2 quarters to decorate muffins. Sift flour, add sugar and make a well in the centre. Beat together eggs, butter and milk, and pour mixture into the well. Fold until just combined, then fold in dried pear, pecans and chopped pear. Divide the mixture among 12 greased muffin holes and decorate with slices of pear. Cook in oven 25-30 minutes or until cooked when tested by skewer.

Golden caramel: Dissolve sugar in the water over low heat, then rapidly boil for about 6 minutes or until mixture is a golden colour. Remove from heat and carefully stir in another 80ml (1/3 cup) water (be careful: this will spit, so protect your hands and arms). Remove muffins from pan and serve drizzled with caramel.

makes 12

muffins

double chocolate muffins

plum and polenta muffins

pear muffins with golden caramel

desserts

amaretti and glacé fruit cassata

per serving 10.1g fat; 1618kJ

1 litre	low-fat ice-cream
90g	glacé pineapple, chopped
120g	glacé peaches, chopped
100g	glacé cherries, chopped
40g	pistachios, toasted and chopped
2 tbsps	Grand Marnier
50g	amaretti biscuits, crushed

Allow ice-cream to soften slightly, mix remaining ingredients through the ice-cream. Spoon into 2-litre loaf tin or terrine which has been rinsed with cold water but not dried.

Tap the container firmly against a bench top, to rid it of any air pockets, and smooth over the top. Cover with plastic wrap and foil and freeze overnight. Remove cassata from freezer, dip base of tin in warm water and turn out onto serving plate. Slice and serve immediately.

NB: Individual portions can be placed on an oven tray and returned to the freezer for later use.

serves 8

"Almost every person has something secret he likes to eat."

M. F. K. FISHER

poached pears
with rosewater and nougat ricotta

per serving 5.7g fat; 1975kJ

750ml	(3 cups) water
375ml	(1½ cups) dry red wine
80ml	(⅓ cup) Drambuie or orange juice
385g	(1¾ cups) caster sugar
1	vanilla bean, split
6	medium pears

rosewater and nougat ricotta

2 tsps	rosewater
200g	(1 cup) reduced-fat ricotta
50g	nougat, chopped

Combine water, wine, liqueur, sugar and vanilla bean in medium pan, stir over low heat until sugar is dissolved. Simmer, uncovered, about 10 minutes or until thickened slightly. Meanwhile, using vegetable peeler, peel thin spiral strips from pears. Add pears to syrup, simmer, uncovered, about 15 minutes or until tender. Cool pears in syrup. Serve warm or cold with rosewater and nougat ricotta.

Rosewater and nougat ricotta: Beat rosewater and ricotta in small bowl with electric mixer until smooth, stir in nougat.

serves 6

Unlike most fruit, pears improve in both texture and flavour after being picked while still hard. They should be stored at room temperature until ripe, then refrigerated. In the 8th century BC, Homer, the Greek poet, referred to pears as "a gift of the gods".

Two small mandarins will supply 35% of the recommended daily allowance of vitamin C. The fruit is also a good source of dietary fibre. Select mandarins that are glossy and heavy for their size, and refrigerate in the crisper for up to 1 week.

baked ricotta
with caramelised mandarins

per serving 8.8g fat; 1062kJ

35g	(½ cup) fine fresh wholemeal breadcrumbs
600g	reduced-fat ricotta cheese, drained
55g	(¼ cup) caster sugar
3	eggs, separated
1 tbsp	finely grated lemon rind
75g	(½ cup) dried currants
4	large (1kg) mandarins, peeled
75g	(⅓ cup) firmly packed brown sugar
1 tbsp	lemon juice

Lightly grease 20cm-round spring-form pan; sprinkle base and sides with breadcrumbs. Combine ricotta, sugar, yolks and rind in a medium bowl; mix until smooth. Stir in currants.

Beat egg whites in a small bowl with electric mixer until stiff peaks form; fold into ricotta mixture. Pour ricotta mixture into prepared pan, bake in moderate oven (180°C) about 50 minutes or until cooked when tested and firm to touch.

Meanwhile, combine mandarins, brown sugar and juice in a medium heavy-based pan; cook over high heat for 4 minutes or until sugar caramelises.

Serve baked ricotta with caramelised mandarins.

serves 8

candied orange rice creams

per serving 3g fat; 1561kJ

150g	(3/4 cup) calrose rice
430ml	(1 3/4 cups) milk
250ml	(1 cup) skim milk
2 tbsps	finely grated orange rind
110g	(1/2 cup) caster sugar

candied orange peel

2	small (360g) oranges, scrubbed
pinch	bicarbonate of soda
220g	(1 cup) caster sugar
330ml	(1 1/3 cups) water

Place rice in small bowl, cover with cold water, stand for 30 minutes; drain. Combine milks, rind and sugar in small pan. Stir over low heat until sugar is dissolved, bring to boil. Remove from heat. Divide rice between 6 x 160ml (2/3 cup) moulds, top with milk mixture. Bake in bain-marie in moderate oven (180°C) for 1 hour or until rice is tender and liquid is almost absorbed. Serve rice creams topped with candied orange peel.

Candied orange peel: Cut oranges into quarters, remove pulp, chop and place in bowl to one side, remove as much of the white pith as possible from the peel, discard. Slice peel into strips and add to large pan of cold water with soda. Bring to boil, simmer 5 minutes, drain and rinse under cold water. Combine sugar and the water in medium pan. Bring to boil, stirring until sugar is dissolved. Add peel and chopped pulp to pan, simmer for 40 minutes or until mixture has thickened and peel is translucent.

serves 6

chocolate mousse tart

per serving 8.5g fat; 783kJ

110g	(3/4 cup) plain flour
1 tbsp	cocoa
2 tbsps	caster sugar
30g	butter
30g	reduced-fat margarine
1	egg yolk

chocolate mousse

2 tsps	powdered gelatine
1 tbsp	boiling water
35g	light milk chocolate, melted
2 tsps	cocoa, sifted
1 tbsp	Tia Maria
60ml	(1/4 cup) light sour cream
60ml	(1/4 cup) low-fat plain yogurt
2	egg whites
1 1/2 tbsps	caster sugar

Grease a 20cm loose-bottomed flan tin. Sift flour, cocoa and sugar into large bowl, rub in butter and margarine until mixture resembles coarse breadcrumbs, add egg yolk and stir until mixture forms a soft dough. Wrap dough in cling wrap, refrigerate for 30 minutes or until firm. Roll pastry between two pieces of baking paper, until pastry is large enough to fit tin. Place pastry in tin and trim excess. Prick base with fork. Bake blind*.

Chocolate mousse: Add gelatine to the boiling water, stir until gelatine is dissolved. Combine gelatine, chocolate, cocoa, Tia Maria, sour cream and yogurt in large bowl. Beat egg whites with electric mixer until soft peaks form, gradually add caster sugar, beating until dissolved between each addition. Gently fold egg whites into chocolate mixture until well combined. Pour into chocolate pastry case, refrigerate for 1 hour, or until set, before cutting.

If you wish, the tart can be decorated with sugared violets.

Baking blind: cut a sheet of baking paper about 5cm larger than flan tin. Cover pastry with paper, fill with dried beans or rice, place on oven tray. Bake in moderate oven (180°C) for 20 minutes. Remove paper and beans carefully from pastry case, bake further 10 minutes; cool.

serves 8

Sugared violets can be bought at specialty chocolate shops and some delicatessens. They're also easy to make: gently wash and dry fresh violets, brush them with lightly beaten egg white and dust with caster sugar. Place on greaseproof paper to dry.

vanilla bean ice-cream

per serving 9.5g fat; 705kJ

125ml **(½ cup) milk**
375ml **(1½ cups) skim milk**
2 **vanilla beans, split**
4 **egg yolks**
110g **(½ cup) caster sugar**
125ml **(½ cup) thickened cream**

Place milks in medium pan, scrape seeds from vanilla beans, add seeds and pods to milk. Bring to boil, remove from heat. Remove pods. Whisk yolks and sugar in small bowl until pale and thick; gradually whisk in hot milk. Stir over heat, without boiling, about 15 minutes or until mixture thickens slightly; remove from heat; cool. Stir in cream. Churn in ice-cream maker, following instructions.

If you don't have an ice-cream maker: Pour mixture into 23cm-square cake pan, cover with foil, freeze 3 hours or until just firm. Remove from pan, beat ice-cream in large bowl with electric mixer until smooth. Return ice-cream to pan, cover, freeze until firm.

serves 8

"My advice to you is not to inquire why or whither, but just enjoy your ice cream while it's on your plate — that's my philosophy."

THORNTON WILDER

winter fruits and lemon grass
grilled with a palm sugar and star anise syrup

per serving 0.5g fat; 959kJ

125ml	(½ cup) red wine
1	vanilla bean, split
200g	(¾ cup) finely chopped palm sugar
160ml	(⅔ cup) water
¼ cup	thinly sliced fresh lemon grass
6	star anise
6	small (1kg) pears*
4	(520g) Lady Finger bananas, halved
2	large (1kg) Ruby Red grapefruit, peeled, thickly sliced
2	large (600g) oranges, peeled, thickly sliced

Combine wine, vanilla bean, sugar, the water, lemon grass and anise in small pan; cook, stirring, until sugar dissolves.

Add pears (pan needs to be small enough for pears to stand upright and close together); simmer, uncovered, about 15 minutes or until pears are just tender. Remove pears from pan; bring syrup to boil; simmer, uncovered, until syrup has reduced by half.

Place pears, banana, grapefruit and orange in large baking dish; drizzle with a little syrup. Cook under hot grill about 5 minutes or until fruit is lightly browned.

Serve fruit drizzled with remaining syrup.

We used two pear varieties – Corella and Beurre Bosc.

serves 6

*"The pedigree of honey
Does not concern the bee;
A clover, any time, to him
Is aristocracy."*

EMILY DICKINSON

strawberries
dipped in lavender honey toffee

per serving 0.1g fat; 1041kJ

440g	(2 cups) raw sugar
125ml	(½ cup) lavender honey*
60ml	(¼ cup) water
1.25kg	strawberries

Combine sugar, honey and the water in small pan; stir over low heat until sugar dissolves. Bring to boil, boil about 5 minutes or until golden brown (or hard crack stage on a candy thermometer).

Place a strawberry on the end of a wooden skewer and quickly dip ⅔ of the strawberry into the toffee. Place strawberry on baking-paper-lined oven tray, gently remove skewer. Repeat with remaining strawberries. If toffee becomes firm, return pan to low heat until toffee melts.

* You can find lavender honey (produced by bees fed on lavender) at selected delicatessens. If unavailable, any variety of honey can be substituted.

serves 10

coffee and cookie gelato

per serving 6.6g fat; 805kJ (825kJ if you don't have an ice-cream maker)

125ml	(½ cup) milk
375ml	(1½ cups) skim milk
1 tbsp	coffee granules
4	egg yolks
110g	(½ cup) caster sugar
3	plain chocolate biscuits
3	egg whites (if you don't have an ice-cream maker)

Combine milks and coffee in large heavy-based pan; stir over low heat until hot; do not boil. Whisk yolks and sugar in medium heatproof bowl until creamy; gradually whisk in hot milk mixture. Place bowl over pan of simmering water; stir over heat, without boiling, about 15 minutes or until mixture coats the back of a spoon. Remove from heat; cool.

Pour mixture into ice-cream maker, churn following manufacturer's instructions. Crumble biscuits into gelato when almost frozen.

If you don't have an ice-cream maker: Pour mixture into a deep, 19cm-square cake pan, cover with foil; freeze 3 hours or until firm. Remove from pan, beat gelato in large bowl with electric mixer until smooth and creamy. Fold in 3 firmly beaten egg whites and crumbled biscuits, return to pan, freeze until firm.

serves 6

lemon, passionfruit and strawberry sorbets
in a mango soup

per serving 1g fat; 7144kJ (7262kJ if you don't have an ice-cream maker)

lemon sorbet

770g	(3¹⁄₂ cups) caster sugar
750ml	(3 cups) water
750ml	(3 cups) fresh lemon juice
¹⁄₄ cup	finely grated lemon rind
4	egg whites (if you don't have an ice-cream maker)

passionfruit sorbet

770g	(3¹⁄₂ cups) caster sugar
750ml	(3 cups) water
750ml	(3 cups) fresh passionfruit pulp
4	egg whites (if you don't have an ice-cream maker)

strawberry sorbet

750g	strawberries
770g	(3¹⁄₂ cups) caster sugar
500ml	(2 cups) water
4	egg whites (if you don't have an ice-cream maker)

mango soup

2	large (1.2kg) mangoes
80ml	(¹⁄₃ cup) sparkling mineral water
2 tbsps	caster sugar
1 tbsp	orange-flavoured liqueur

Lemon sorbet: Combine sugar and the water in medium pan; stir over heat, without boiling, until sugar is dissolved. Simmer, uncovered, about 10 minutes or until mixture begins to thicken slightly; cool. Stir in juice and rind. Pour mixture into ice-cream maker, churn following manufacturer's instructions.

If you don't have an ice-cream maker: Freeze lemon mixture in a 20cm x 30cm lamington pan, until firm. Remove mixture from pan, beat with electric mixer until thick and fluffy. Return mixture to pan, freeze until firm. Remove from pan, beat with electric mixer, adding 4 egg whites, one at a time, beating until fluffy. Pour lemon mixture into 15cm x 25cm loaf pan, freeze until firm.

Passionfruit sorbet: Combine sugar and the water in medium pan; stir over heat, without boiling, until sugar is dissolved. Simmer, uncovered, about 10 minutes or until mixture begins to thicken slightly; cool. Stir in pulp. Pour mixture into ice-cream maker, churn following manufacturer's instructions.

If you don't have an ice-cream maker: Follow same method as for lemon sorbet.

Strawberry sorbet: Blend or process strawberries until nearly smooth; strain. Proceed as for passionfruit sorbet method, adding strawberry puree in place of passionfruit.

If you don't have an ice-cream maker: Follow same method as for lemon sorbet.

Serve lemon, passionfruit and strawberry sorbets with mango soup.

Mango soup: Peel mangoes and slice off cheeks. Blend or process mango, the water and sugar until just combined. Stir in liqueur, if desired.

serves 6

grapefruit and campari granita

per serving 0.2g fat; 603kJ

110g	(½ cup) caster sugar
250ml	(1 cup) water
2 tbsps	finely grated ruby red or pink grapefruit rind
1 litre	(4 cups) ruby red or pink grapefruit juice, strained
125ml	(½ cup) Campari

Combine sugar and the water in large pan, stirring over heat, without boiling, until sugar dissolves. Bring to boil, boil 3 minutes or until slightly thickened, remove from heat; cool.

Stir rind, juice and Campari into sugar mixture. Pour into a shallow pan, cover with foil; freeze until firm. Stir occasionally with a fork during freezing. Shave granita into individual glasses to serve.

serves 6

nectarines with almond crumble

per serving 3.8g fat; 653kJ

4	**large (500g) ripe nectarines**
2 tbsps	**plain flour**
¼ tsp	**ground cinnamon**
20g	**low-fat margarine**
1½ tbsps	**brown sugar**
25g	**(¼ cup) muesli**
1½ tbsps	**flaked almonds**
125ml	**(½ cup) dessert wine**

Preheat oven to moderate (190°C). Halve and deseed unpeeled nectarines. Combine flour and cinnamon in a small bowl, rub in margarine. Stir in sugar, muesli and almonds, spoon on top of each nectarine, cut side up. Place in a pie plate. Pour wine around the base, bake for 15 minutes or until nectarines are soft and topping is lightly browned.

serves 4

chocolate puddings

per serving 3.4g fat; 1294kJ

150g	(1 cup) self-raising flour
165g	(¾ cup) caster sugar
2 tbsps	cocoa
125ml	(½ cup) skim milk
30g	reduced-fat margarine, melted
60g	nougat, chopped
75g	(⅓ cup) firmly packed brown sugar
250ml	(1 cup) hot water

Spray 6 x 180ml (¾-cup) ramekins with cooking oil spray. Sift flour, caster sugar and cocoa into large bowl; add milk, margarine and nougat, stir until well combined. Divide chocolate mixture between ramekins and sprinkle brown sugar over tops. Place ramekins in baking dish, pour the hot water around the puddings. Bake, uncovered, in moderate oven (180°C) for 35 minutes or until puddings are cooked when tested.

serves 6

caramelised quince
with honey and nougat

per serving 0.5g fat; 3540kJ

440g	(2 cups) raw sugar
875ml	(3½ cups) water
1	vanilla bean, split
125ml	(½ cup) red wine
60ml	(¼ cup) lemon juice
3	medium (990g) quince, thickly sliced
250ml	(1 cup) honey
50g	almond nougat, roughly chopped

Combine sugar, water, vanilla, wine and half of the juice in large saucepan, stir over low heat until sugar is dissolved. Bring to boil, add quince; simmer, uncovered, about 35 minutes or until quince is deep red in colour, cooked through, and syrup has thickened.

Just before serving, stir in honey and remaining juice.

Serve sprinkled with nougat.

serves 4

The quince was a favoured fruit of the Ancient Romans, who called it the golden apple. The Romans spread the custom of giving newlyweds a quince as a symbol of good luck before they crossed the threshold of their new home.

apple galette
with raisin caramel

per serving 14g fat; 3128kJ

9	small apples
295g	(1¹⁄₃ cups) caster sugar
2	cinnamon sticks
2 tbsps	grated lime rind
80ml	(¹⁄₃ cup) lime juice
2	sheets (24cm x 24cm) puff pastry
2 tbsps	skim milk
1 tbsp	granulated sugar

raisin caramel

275g	(1¹⁄₄ cups) caster sugar
15g	reduced-fat margarine
100g	raisins

Halve apples lengthways, peel, then scoop out cores with a teaspoon. Place apples, sugar, cinnamon, rind and juice in a medium pan. Barely cover with cold water, cover pan and slowly bring to a simmer for about 15 minutes. Remove pan from heat and allow apples to cool to room temperature. Strain apples and reserve the liquid, discard cinnamon sticks and rind.

Place each sheet of pastry on a lightly greased baking tray. Brush each sheet all over with a little of the skim milk. Roll up the sides of each pastry sheet 3cm. Divide apple halves, cut side up, between pastry sheets. Brush sides of pastry with remaining skim milk, sprinkle pastry and apples with granulated sugar. Bake in moderately hot oven (200°C) for 40 minutes or until pastry is golden brown. Serve apple galette with raisin caramel and toffee pieces.

Raisin caramel: Place 55g (¹⁄₄ cup) of the sugar into a heavy-based pan and cook over a medium heat until it caramelises. Pour onto a lightly oiled baking tray. Break into small pieces when set. Place remaining sugar in small pan and cook over medium heat until it caramelises. Stir in 250ml (1 cup) of reserved apple cooking liquid, then swirl in the margarine and raisins. Simmer for 5 minutes or until caramel is slightly thickened.

serves 6

golden syrup
orange steamed puddings

per serving 6g fat; 1685kJ

40g	reduced-fat margarine
110g	(½ cup) sugar
1	egg
1	egg white
185g	(1¼ cups) self-raising flour
pinch	salt
1 tbsp	finely grated orange rind
60ml	(¼ cup) skim milk
250ml	(1 cup) golden syrup

Beat margarine and sugar in small bowl with electric mixer until combined. Add egg and egg white, one at a time, beat until mixture is pale and fluffy. Stir in flour, salt, rind and milk.

Lightly grease 6 x 180ml (¾-cup) ramekins. Line each ramekin with 2 tbsps golden syrup. Spoon batter into ramekins, cover tightly with foil.

Place ramekins in large pan of boiling water (water should come halfway up sides of ramekins), cover pan with tight-fitting lid; simmer about 45 minutes.

Turn puddings out onto serving plate; top with candied orange as pictured, if desired.

serves 6

grilled tamarillos
with fresh honeycomb

per serving 0.1g fat; 575kJ

55g	(¼ cup) caster sugar
60ml	(¼ cup) water
1 tbsp	madeira
8	tamarillos, halved
40g	fresh honeycomb, chopped

Combine sugar, the water and madeira in small pan. Simmer, stirring, without boiling, until sugar is dissolved. Boil gently for 3 minutes or until slightly thickened. Brush cut side of tamarillos with a little of the sugar syrup, place cut side down on oiled barbecue bars. Cook for 1 minute or until slightly softened. Serve drizzled with remaining sugar syrup and topped with fresh honeycomb.

NB: Fresh honeycomb is available from speciality food stores and good delicatessens.

serves 4

chocolate and coffee panforte

per slice 1.6g fat; 604kJ

4	sheets confectionery rice paper
165g	(3/4 cup) raw sugar
80g	(1/2 cup) glucose
2 tbsps	water
100g	dark chocolate Melts
2 tbsps	kirsch
2 tsps	instant coffee
1 tbsp	hot water
300g	glacé cherries, halved
200g	chopped glacé orange peel
110g	(3/4 cup) plain flour
1 tbsp	cocoa

Preheat oven to moderately slow (170°C). Cut rice paper to fit the base of a 29cm x 19cm rectangular slice pan. Place 2 sheets on the base, set remaining 2 sheets aside.

Combine sugar, glucose and the water in medium pan, stir over high heat until sugar has dissolved. Bring to boil, reduce heat to low, cook, without stirring, for 5 minutes or until a teaspoonful of mixture will set to a soft toffee consistency when placed in a glass of cold water; swirl pan occasionally.

Melt dark chocolate Melts in a bowl over a saucepan of boiling water (or microwave on HIGH about 1 minute). Combine kirsch, combined coffee and hot water, cherries, peel and sifted flour and cocoa. Add toffee mixture and chocolate, stir until combined. Carefully spread mixture over the rice paper, press reserved rice paper firmly over the top. Bake for 30 minutes, allow to cool in the tin. Run a knife around the pan, turn out, refrigerate until firm. Cut into squares.

NB: Confectionery rice paper sheets are the variety that do not need soaking in water. They are available from delicatessens, health food stores, Asian food stores and some supermarkets.

makes 20 slices

sesame caramels

per square 2.8g fat; 262kJ

400g	condensed milk
2 tbsps	golden syrup
40g	copha
1 tbsp	sesame seeds

Grease a 25cm x 8cm bar tin, line base and sides with baking paper. Combine condensed milk and golden syrup in a medium saucepan. Stir constantly over medium heat for 10 minutes or until mixture turns a light golden brown. It may be necessary to reduce the heat gradually as the caramel is cooking to prevent burning. Remove from the heat, stir in copha and sesame seeds. Spread into prepared tin, press down with wet fingers, allow to cool. Remove from tin, cut into squares.

makes 30 squares

almond fruit bread

per slice 0.8g fat; 262kJ

3	egg whites
110g	(1/2 cup) caster sugar
150g	(1 cup) plain flour
40g	(1/4 cup) almond kernels, halved
100g	glacé red cherries, sliced
60g	glacé pineapple, chopped
60g	glacé apricots, chopped

Grease 25cm x 8cm bar tin.

Beat egg whites until soft peaks form, gradually beat in sugar, beating well after each addition until all sugar is dissolved. Fold in sifted flour, almonds and fruit.

Spread mixture into prepared tin. Bake in moderate oven (180°C) about 30 minutes or until firm to touch. Cool on wire rack.

When cold, wrap in foil, stand for 1-2 days. Cut bread into wafer-thin slices; place slices on oven trays, bake in slow oven (150°C) about 45 minutes or until dry and crisp.

makes 30 slices

chocolate and coffee panforte

sesame caramels

almond fruit bread

breakfasts and drinks

apple and watermelon slush

per serving 0.6g fat; 797kJ

2	**large (400g) Granny Smith apples**
500g	**chopped watermelon with seeds removed**
8	**mint leaves**
2 tbsps	**Cointreau, optional**
	Ice

Peel, core and chop apples. Combine in a blender with watermelon, blend until smooth. Add mint and Cointreau (if using), blend until mint is finely chopped. Pour into glasses of ice.

serves 2

Granny Smith apples were first grown by Maria Anne Smith, in Sydney, Australia, in 1867. They are now one of the major apple varieties grown around the world.

roasted corn frittata
with smoked salmon

per serving 4.9g fat; 594kJ

420g	can corn kernels, drained well
1/2	small (100g) leek, thinly sliced
1	clove garlic, crushed
4	eggs, lightly beaten
4	egg whites, lightly beaten
125ml	(1/2 cup) skim milk
100g	sliced smoked salmon
1/4 cup	fresh dill tips

Heat a 24cm non-stick pan; cook corn until lightly browned. Add leek and garlic; cook, stirring, until leek is soft. Remove half the corn mixture from pan, reserve.

Whisk eggs, egg whites and milk in small bowl. Pour half the egg mixture into pan with corn mixture; cook over medium heat until egg mixture is almost set. Place pan under heated grill until top is set and lightly browned. Repeat with remaining corn mixture and egg mixture.

Serve frittata with salmon and dill.

serves 6

Corn is one of the few vegetables that, along with potatoes and kumara, is a good source of starchy carbohydrates. It is also high in dietary fibre, folate and potassium, as well as containing vitamin C, beta-carotene and niacin.

mango **smoothie**

per serving 1.8g fat; 1519kJ

1	**ripe medium (430g) mango, peeled, cut in chunks**
150ml	**can light evaporated milk, chilled**
1	**scoop low-fat ice-cream**
1 tbsp	**icing sugar**
	Crushed ice cubes
	Mint leaves, optional

Place all ingredients except mint in blender, blend until thick and creamy. Pour into serving glasses, top with mint leaves.

serves 1

honey toasted granola
with raspberries

per serving 8.3g fat; 2067kJ

15g	(¼ cup) shredded coconut
360g	(4 cups) rolled oats
20g	(¼ cup) bran cereal
2 tbsps	unsalted sunflower seeds
2 tbsps	pumpkin seeds
½ tsp	sesame seeds
½ tsp	ground cinnamon
170g	(1 cup) raisins
400g	(1½ cups) honey
1 litre	(4 cups) skim milk
300g	raspberries

Combine coconut, oats, bran, seeds, cinnamon, raisins and honey in large bowl; mix well. Spread mixture over 2 lightly oiled baking dishes. Bake in moderate oven (180°C) about 30 minutes, stirring occasionally, or until golden brown. Cool. Serve granola with skim milk and raspberries.

serves 8

It takes 250 bees four weeks to collect enough nectar to make 500g of honey.

caramelised apple
fruit toast

per serving 4.6g fat; 1485kJ

165g	(3/4 cup) raw sugar
60ml	(1/4 cup) apple juice
3	small (390g) red apples, cored, cut into wedges
60g	(1/4 cup) light cream cheese
50g	(1/4 cup) low-fat ricotta
1	vanilla bean, split, or 1/2 tsp vanilla extract
1½ tbsps	icing sugar mixture
12	thick slices fruit bread, toasted

Place sugar in heavy-based pan; stir over medium heat 5 minutes or until sugar dissolves. Simmer, uncovered, stirring occasionally, about 3 minutes or until sugar changes colour to caramel.

Add apple juice and apple (carefully, as toffee may spit); simmer, uncovered, stirring occasionally, until apple is tender and syrup is thickened.

Combine cream cheese, ricotta, vanilla bean and icing sugar in small bowl; beat until smooth.

Spread ricotta mixture on toast, top with apple wedges and drizzle with syrup.

serves 6

*"My wife and I tried to breakfast together,
but we had to stop or our marriage
would have been wrecked."*

WINSTON CHURCHILL

ham and rocket **bread pudding**

per serving 6.1g fat; 1213kJ

450g	unsliced grain bread
375ml	(1½ cups) skim milk
1	small (80g) onion, chopped
1	clove garlic, crushed
250g	button mushrooms, sliced
250g	rocket, chopped
100g	low-fat sliced breakfast ham, chopped
3	medium (570g) vine-ripened tomatoes, chopped
3	eggs, lightly beaten
3	egg whites, lightly beaten

Grease a 24cm-square slab cake pan.

Cut bread into 2cm cubes. Combine bread and milk in a large bowl; stand 15 minutes. Cook onion, garlic and mushrooms in a large, heated, oiled pan, stirring, until mushrooms are tender and liquid is evaporated.

Combine onion mixture in large bowl with bread, rocket, ham and tomatoes; spoon into prepared pan. Pour combined eggs and egg whites over bread mixture. Bake in moderate oven (180°C) 40 minutes or until cooked when tested.

serves 6

latte coffee

per serving 3.7g fat; 754kJ

30g	**(⅓ cup) coarsely ground coffee beans**
½	**vanilla bean, split in half**
500ml	**(2 cups) low-fat milk**
1 tbsp	**Tia Maria**

Combine coffee, vanilla bean and milk in a medium saucepan, cook over low heat until heated through, but not boiling. Pour through a fine strainer into serving glasses, stir in Tia Maria.

Hint: Float a few extra whole coffee beans in the glass for serving – this is for decoration only, not for eating.

serves 2

bran muffins

per muffin 9.5g fat; 1146kJ

210g	(3 cups) All-Bran
250ml	(1 cup) boiling water
220g	(1 cup) caster sugar
2	eggs
125ml	(½ cup) vegetable oil
500ml	(2 cups) skim milk
2 tbsps	lemon juice
375g	(2½ cups) plain flour
2½ tsps	bicarbonate of soda

Preheat oven to moderately hot (200°C). Combine 70g (1 cup) All-Bran with the water, set aside. Combine sugar, eggs and oil in a large bowl, whisk until smooth. Add milk and lemon juice, whisk until combined. Add All-Bran mixture, remaining dry All-Bran and sifted flour and soda, stir until combined.

Spoon mixture into greased 180ml (¾-cup) muffin tins. Bake for 20 minutes or until golden brown.

makes 15

spiced chocolate milk

per serving 11g fat; 1095kJ

8 squares dark chocolate
500ml (2 cups) low-fat milk
1 cinnamon stick

Melt chocolate in a cup placed in a saucepan of simmering water or in the microwave. Pour into 2 serving glasses. Use a teaspoon to smear the chocolate up the insides of the glasses. Combine milk and cinnamon stick in a medium saucepan, cook over low heat until heated through, but not boiling. Remove cinnamon. Pour milk into chocolate-coated glasses. Sprinkle with shaved chocolate, if desired.

Hint: A liqueur-flavoured chocolate tastes great.

serves 2

"Thought: Why does man kill? He kills for food. And not only food: frequently there must be a beverage."
WOODY ALLEN

quick mix
banana soy
muffins

per muffin 6g fat; 1121kJ

300g	(2 cups) self-raising flour
160g	(1 cup) wholemeal self-raising flour
1/2 tsp	bicarbonate of soda
100g	(1/2 cup) firmly packed brown sugar
80g	(1/2 cup) finely chopped seeded dried dates
1 cup	mashed very ripe banana
70g	(1/4 cup) honey
60ml	(1/4 cup) vegetable oil
125ml	(1/2 cup) low-fat soy milk
1	egg

Grease 12-hole (80ml/1/3-cup capacity) muffin pan. Sift flours, soda and sugar into large bowl; stir in dates, banana, honey, oil, milk and egg; do not overmix, mixture should look coarse and lumpy. Spoon mixture into prepared pan. Bake in moderately hot oven (200°C) about 25 minutes.

makes 12

raspberry and watermelon **frappé**

per cup 0.6g fat; 398kJ

½ **small (2.25kg)**
watermelon, chopped

600g **raspberries**

500ml **(2 cups) chilled apple juice**

½ cup **firmly packed fresh**
mint leaves

Blend or process all ingredients until smooth; serve over crushed ice.

makes about 8 cups

*"I can't get cool.
I've drunk a quantity of lemonade.
I think I'll take my shoes off
And sit around in the shade."*

SHEL SILVERSTEIN

lemonade

per serving 0.02g fat; 575kJ

4	**medium (560g) lemons**
880g	**(4 cups) sugar**
500ml	**(2 cups) water**
	Mineral water

Remove rind from lemons using a vegetable peeler, avoiding white pith; reserve lemons. Combine rind, sugar and the water in large pan; stir over low heat, without boiling, until sugar is dissolved. Bring to boil, simmer, uncovered, without stirring, about 10 minutes or until syrup is thickened slightly; cool.

Squeeze juice from lemons (you will need 250ml/1 cup juice). Add juice to syrup, strain into jug; cover, keep refrigerated.

Just before serving, add 4 parts mineral water to 1 part lemonade, or to taste.

NB: This recipe can be made up to 1 week ahead, keep refrigerated.

makes about 1.25 litres undiluted lemonade (25 serves diluted)

glossary

all-bran breakfast cereal based on wheat bran.

amaretti biscuits small, Italian-style macaroons based on ground almonds.

baking powder a raising agent consisting mainly of two parts cream of tartar to one part bicarbonate of soda (baking soda).

bean sprouts also known as bean shoots; new growths of assorted germinated beans and seeds.

beans
black also known as turtle beans or black kidney beans; earthy-flavoured dried bean different from the better-known Chinese black beans.
broad also known as fava beans; available fresh, canned or frozen. Best when peeled twice (discard the long pod and pale-green inner shell).
butter also known as lima beans; available both dried and canned, butter beans are large and beige with a mealy texture and mild taste.
cannellini small dried white bean similar to great northern and navy or haricot beans.

beetroot also known as red beets or, simply, beets; round root vegetable with deep-pink flesh.

blood orange juicy citrus fruit with red flesh.

blood plum round fruit with deep-red flesh.

bok choy also known as pak choi or Chinese white cabbage; has fresh, mild mustard taste. Baby bok choy is more delicate in flavour.

breadcrumbs
packaged fine-textured, crunchy, purchased white breadcrumbs.
stale one- or two-day old bread made into crumbs by grating, blending or processing.

buckwheat the triangular seeds of an annual plant; used in the same way as cereal grains.

burghul also known as bulghur; dried, steamed wheat kernels crushed into small grains.

butter 125g is equal to one stick butter; available salted or unsalted (sweet).

buttermilk commercially made by a method similar to yogurt, buttermilk is low in fat.

campari Italian aperitif with a strong bitter taste.

caper berries fruit formed after the caper buds have flowered.

capers the green buds of a warm-climate shrub; sold either dried and salted, or pickled.

capsicum also known as bell pepper or pepper.

celeriac tuberous root with brown skin, white flesh and celery-like flavour.

cheese
fetta Greek in origin; crumbly textured goat- or sheep-milk cheese with a sharp, salty taste.
gruyère Swiss cheese with nutty flavour.
low-fat cheddar common cow milk cheese with a bite; has fat content of not more than 7%.
low-fat fetta fetta cheese with average fat content of 15%.
low-fat ricotta unripened cheese made from whey.
parmesan sharp-tasting, hard cheese made from skim or part-skim milk and aged at least a year.

chestnut puree unsweetened puree of chestnuts; do not confuse with sweetened chestnut spread.

chickpeas also known as garbanzos, hummus or channa; round, sandy-coloured legumes.

chillies
birdseye small chilli with deep, fiery heat.
sweet chilli sauce mild, Thai-type sauce made from red chillies, sugar, garlic and vinegar.
thai small chilli that is medium-hot and bright-red to dark-green in colour.

chinese barbecued pork also known as char siew; has sweet-sticky coating and is available from Asian food stores.

chinese broccoli also known as gai lum.

chinese cabbage also known as Peking cabbage or wong bok.

chinese five-spice fragrant mixture of ground cinnamon, cloves, star anise, Sichuan pepper and fennel seeds.

chinese spinach also known as amaranth or yin choy; sold with pinkish-red roots intact.

chorizo sausage pork sausage of Spanish origin; seasoned with garlic and chilli.

choy sum also known as flowering bok choy or flowering white cabbage.

ciabatta crusty, slightly sour-tasting Italian bread.

coconut milk, light reduced-fat coconut milk available in cans.

cointreau an orange-flavoured liqueur.

condensed milk canned milk product with over half of water content removed and sugar added.

copha solid white shortening based on coconut oil.

coriander also known as cilantro or Chinese parsley; leafy herb with pungent flavour – sold with roots intact. Also available ground or in seed form.

cornflour also known as cornstarch.

couscous fine, grain-like cereal product; made from semolina.

cream cheese, low-fat low-fat version of soft milk cheese commonly known as "Philadelphia".

cream of tartar acid ingredient in baking powder; added to help prevent sugar crystallising.

cream, light sour contains minimum fat content of 18%; commercially cultured soured cream.

curly endive also known as frisee; curly-leafed green vegetable.

curry paste, red commercially made curry paste available in supermarkets.

curry powder commercial blend of spices; can consist of: dried chilli, cinnamon, coriander, cumin, fennel, fenugreek, mace, cardamom, turmeric.

daikon also known as a giant white radish.

drambuie a liqueur based on Scotch and honey.

eggplant also known as aubergine.

fennel also known as finocchio or anise; also the name given to dried seeds with a licorice flavour.

filo pastry also known as phylo; tissue-thin pastry sheets purchased from supermarkets.

fish sauce also known as nam pla or nuoc nam; made from pulverised, fermented fish.

flour
plain an all-purpose flour made from wheat.
rice fine flour made from ground white rice.
soy flour made from ground soy beans.
wholemeal plain all-purpose wholewheat flour.
self-raising plain flour sifted with baking powder in the proportion of 2 teaspoons baking powder to 1 cup flour.

garam masala blend of roasted, ground spices, in varying proportions, consisting of: cardamom, cinnamon, cloves, coriander, cumin and fennel.

garlic chives herb with long, flat leaves.

gelatine also spelled gelatin; a thickening agent which is available in powder and sheet form.

golden syrup by-product of refined sugarcane.

gow gee wrappers wonton, spring roll or egg pastry sheets can be substituted.

grand marnier orange-flavoured liqueur.

grapefruit, ruby red ruby red grapefruit have juicy pink-red flesh and are sweeter than yellow varieties.

harissa paste made from dried red chillies, garlic, oil and sometimes caraway seeds.

hoisin sauce thick, sweet and spicy Chinese paste made from fermented soy beans.

kaffir lime leaves aromatic leaves of small citrus tree; use fresh or dried.

kalamata olives large, plump variety of black olive.

ketjap manis sweet Indonesian soy sauce.

kirsch clear fruit brandy distilled from cherries.

kumara Polynesian name of orange-fleshed sweet potato often confused with yam.

laksa paste commercially prepared paste.

lamb's lettuce also known as mâche or corn salad; leafy green lettuce.

lemon grass lemon-smelling and -tasting grass; white lower part of each stem is used in cooking.

lemon pepper commercial blend of cracked black pepper, lemon, herbs and spices.

liquid glucose also known as glucose syrup; available from health food stores and supermarkets.

macadamia nuts rich, buttery Australian nut; store in refrigerator because of high oil content.

madeira fortified wine that originated in Portugal.

maple syrup distilled sap of the maple tree.

margarine, reduced-fat polyunsaturated spread with a reduced fat content.

milk
low-fat soy a non-dairy milk substitute.
skim milk with 0.1% fat content.

mirin sweet, low-alcohol rice wine.

mushrooms

button small, cultivated white mushrooms with delicate flavour.

enoki tiny white mushroom with long stalks.

field also known as flat mushrooms.

oyster fan-shaped mushroom.

pine also known as matsutake mushrooms; dark brown with thick, meaty stem.

shiitake also known as Chinese black mushrooms; available fresh and dried.

swiss brown also known as portobello mushrooms; light- to dark-brown in colour.

mustard

dijon pale-brown, distinctively flavoured mild French mustard.

dry mustard powder.

seeded also known as wholegrain mustard; coarse-grain mustard made from crushed mustard seeds and Dijon mustard.

seeds seeds are available in black and yellow.

noodles

bean thread also called cellophane; made from green mung bean flour.

chow mein Chinese-style egg noodle.

egg made from wheat flour, water and egg.

hokkien round, medium-thick, yellow egg noodle.

pad thai rice stick noodles; thin dried noodle made from rice flour and water.

rice vermicelli also known as rice-flour noodles; made from ground rice and sold dried.

wheat made from wheat flour.

nori dried seaweed sold in tissue-thin sheets.

oil

canola refined rape-seed oil.

grapeseed can be purchased from most delicatessens; if unavailable, substitute olive oil.

olive made from ripened olives. Extra virgin olive oil and virgin olive oil are the best.

peanut pressed from ground peanuts.

sesame made from roasted, crushed white sesame seeds; used as a flavouring.

vegetable oils sourced from plants, rather than derived from animal fats.

walnut can be purchased from most delicatessens; if unavailable, substitute olive oil.

onion

green also known as scallion or (incorrectly) shallot; onion picked before bulb has formed.

spanish also known as red, red Spanish or Bermuda onion; sweet, large purple-red onion.

spring large sweet white bulb with green stalks.

orange curaçao orange-flavoured liqueur.

osso buco veal knuckle or shank sawn into round, thick pieces.

oyster sauce made from soy sauce, oysters, brine and salt.

pasta

bavette also known as tagliatelle or linguine.

capellini also known as angel hair pasta.

risoni rice-shaped pasta.

pattipan squash also known as scallopini; colour ranges from pale-green to deep yellow.

pawpaw also known as papaya or papaw; large, pear-shaped red-orange tropical fruit.

pepita dried pumpkin seed.

pernod an aniseed-flavoured liqueur.

pickled ginger thinly shaved ginger pickled in a mixture of vinegar, sugar and natural colouring.

pide also known as Turkish bread; comes in long flat loaves or individual rounds.

pimento also known as pimiento; sweet red capsicum preserved in brine in cans or jars.

pine nuts also known as pignoli; small cream-coloured kernels obtained from pine cones.

pistachios pale-green delicately flavoured nut.

pitta bread also known as lebanese or pita bread; pocket bread sold in large, flat pieces.

polenta cereal made of ground corn (maize).

potato

chat also known as baby new potatoes; a potato that has been harvested very young.

kipfler finger-length, nutty-flavoured potato.

sebago white-fleshed potato with creamy skin.

desiree golden-fleshed potato with pink skin.

prawns also known as shrimp.

preserved lemon available from delicatessens; pieces of lemon preserved in a salt mixture.

prosciutto salt-cured, air-dried (unsmoked), pressed ham; usually sold in paper-thin slices.

pumpkin also known as winter squash.

butternut elongated pumpkin with cream skin.

jap large pumpkin with dark-green mottled skin.

queensland blue also known as jarrahdale; large pumpkin with smoky blue-grey skin.

rice

arborio small round-grain rice.

basmati white, fragrant, long-grained rice.

calrose medium-size grain; extremely versatile.

jasmine aromatic long-grain white rice.

paper sheets also known as banh trang; made from rice paste stamped into rounds or squares.

wild distinctively flavoured, blackish-brown seed often sold blended with white rice.

rocket also called arugula, rugula and rucola; peppery-tasting green salad leaf.

rosewater made from crushed rose petals; used for its aromatic quality in many desserts.

saffron threads stigma of variety of crocus; lends yellow-orange colour to food once infused.

salmon roe also known as red caviar; lightly salted fish eggs.

sambal oelek a chilli paste, Indonesian in origin.

shallots, golden also called French shallots or eschalots; small, brown-skinned member of onion family. Grows in tight clusters, like garlic.

sherry, dry a fortified wine.

snake beans very long, thin, round green beans.

snow peas also known as mange tout (eat all). Snow pea tendrils and sprouts are also available.

sourdough bread crunchy, crusted bread with soft inner crumb; has sour flavour.

spatchcock also known as poussin; chicken not more than six weeks old, weighs maximum 500g.

spinach also known as English spinach; leafy green vegetable.

star-anise dried, star-shaped pod, the seeds of which taste of aniseed.

stock available in tetra packs in supermarkets.

sugar

brown soft, fine, granulated sugar retaining molasses for its deep colour and flavour.

caster also known as superfine or finely granulated table sugar.

demerara small-grained golden crystal sugar.

icing sugar mixture also known as confectioners' sugar or powdered sugar.

palm also known as gula jawa, gula melaka and jaggery; very fine sugar from coconut palm.

raw natural, brown, granulated sugar.

sugar snap peas pods with small formed peas inside; they are eaten whole, raw or cooked.

tabasco sauce brand name of fiery sauce.

tahini buttery paste made from sesame seeds.

tamari thick, dark, wheat-free soy sauce.

tangerine citrus fruit; bright-orange to red in colour.

thai basil also known as bai kaprow or holy basil; has small crinkly leaves with strong flavour.

tia maria coffee-flavoured liqueur based on rum.

tikka sauce a packaged Indian-style curry sauce.

tofu also known as bean curd; made from soy "milk", it is available fresh in soft or firm varieties.

tomato

cherry also known as Tiny Tim or Tom Thumb tomatoes; small and round with intense flavour.

egg also known as plum or Roma; oval-shaped.

green unripe tomatoes.

paste triple-concentrated tomato puree.

vanilla bean dried pod containing tiny black seeds.

vietnamese mint also known as Cambodian mint and laksa leaf (daun laksa); pungent herb.

vinegar

apple cider made from fermented apples.

balsamic authentic only from Modena, Italy; made from wine of white Trebbiano grapes.

brown malt made from fermented malt barley and beech shavings.

raspberry made from fresh raspberries steeped in white wine vinegar.

red wine based on red wine.

rice also known as seasoned rice vinegar.

tarragon white wine vinegar with fresh tarragon.

white wine made from white wine.

wasabi paste pungent, fiery green paste made with Asian horseradish.

watercress small, rounded, dark-green leaves with slightly bitter, peppery flavour.

witlof also known as chicory or Belgian endive.

yeast, fresh a fungus which ferments sugars, leading to the leavening of flour mixtures.

zucchini also known as courgette.

index

facts and figures

Wherever you live, you'll be able to use our recipes with the help of these easy-to-follow conversions. While these conversions are approximate only, the difference between an exact and the approximate conversion of various liquid and dry measures is but minimal and will not affect your cooking results.

dry measures

metric	imperial
15g	1/2oz
30g	1oz
60g	2oz
90g	3oz
125g	4oz (1/4lb)
155g	5oz
185g	6oz
220g	7oz
250g	8oz (1/2lb)
280g	9oz
315g	10oz
345g	11oz
375g	12oz (3/4lb)
410g	13oz
440g	14oz
470g	15oz
500g	16oz (1lb)
750g	24oz (1 1/2lb)
1kg	32oz (2lb)

liquid measures

metric	imperial
30ml	1 fluid oz
60ml	2 fluid oz
100ml	3 fluid oz
125ml	4 fluid oz
150ml	5 fluid oz (1/4 pint/1 gill)
190ml	6 fluid oz
250ml	8 fluid oz
300ml	10 fluid oz (1/2 pint)
500ml	16 fluid oz
600ml	20 fluid oz (1 pint)
1000ml (1 litre)	1 3/4 pints

helpful measures

metric	imperial
3mm	1/8in
6mm	1/4in
1cm	1/2in
2cm	3/4in
2.5cm	1in
5cm	2in
6cm	2 1/2in
8cm	3in
10cm	4in
13cm	5in
15cm	6in
18cm	7in
20cm	8in
23cm	9in
25cm	10in
28cm	11in
30cm	12in (1ft)

helpful measures

The difference between one country's measuring cups and another's is, at most, within a 2 or 3 teaspoon variance. (For the record, 1 Australian metric measuring cup holds approximately 250ml.) The most accurate way of measuring dry ingredients is to weigh them. When measuring liquids, use a clear glass or plastic jug with the metric markings. (One Australian metric tablespoon holds 20ml; one Australian metric teaspoon holds 5ml.)

Note: North America, NZ and the UK use 15ml tablespoons. All cup and spoon measurements are level.

We use large eggs having an average weight of 60g.

how to measure

When using graduated metric measuring cups, shake dry ingredients loosely into the appropriate cup. Do not tap the cup on a bench or tightly pack the ingredients unless directed to do so. Level top of measuring cups and measuring spoons with a knife. When measuring liquids, place a clear glass or plastic jug with metric markings on a flat surface to check accuracy at eye level.

oven temperatures

These oven temperatures are only a guide. Always check the manufacturer's manual.

	°C (Celsius)	°F (Fahrenheit)	Gas Mark
Very slow	120	250	1
Slow	150	300	2
Moderately slow	160	325	3
Moderate	180 - 190	350 - 375	4
Moderately hot	200 - 210	400 - 425	5
Hot	220 - 230	450 - 475	6
Very hot	240 - 250	500 - 525	7

Editor *Julie Collard*
Designer *Alison Windmill*
Food editors *Wendy Berecry, Sarah O'Brien*
Photographer *Ashley Mackevicius*
Design consultant *Hieu Nguyen*

Home Library Staff
Editor-in-chief *Mary Coleman*
Managing editor (food) *Susan Tomnay*
Managing editor (general) *Georgina Bitcon*
Senior editor *Liz Neate*
Chief sub-editor *Julie Collard*
Sub-editor *Debbie Quick*
Art director *Michele Withers*
Designers *Mary Keep, Caryl Wiggins, Alison Windmill*
Studio manager *Caryl Wiggins*
Editorial coordinator *Fiona Lambrou*
Book sales manager *Jennifer McDonald*
Publicity and promotions *Johanna Hegerty*

SimplyLite **Staff**
Editor *Sue Wannan*
Creative director *Hieu Nguyen*
Associate editor *Lynda Wilton*

Chief executive officer *John Alexander*
Group publisher *Jill Baker*
Publisher *Sue Wannan*

Produced by *The Australian Women's Weekly*
Home Library, Sydney.
Colour separations by ACP Colour Graphics Pty Ltd,
Sydney. Printing by Dai Nippon Printing in Korea.
Published by ACP Publishing Pty Limited,
54 Park St, Sydney; GPO Box 4088, Sydney, NSW 1028.
Ph: (02) 9282 8618 Fax: (02) 9267 9438.
awwhomelib@acp.com.au
www.awwbooks.com.au

AUSTRALIA: Distributed by Network Distribution
Company, GPO Box 4088, Sydney, NSW 1028.
Ph: (02) 9282 8777 Fax: (02) 9264 3278.
UNITED KINGDOM: Distributed by Australian
Consolidated Press (UK), Moulton Park Business Centre,
Red House Rd, Moulton Park, Northampton, NN3 6AQ
Ph: (01604) 497 531 Fax: (01604) 497 533
acpukltd@aol.com
CANADA: Distributed by Whitecap Books Ltd, 351 Lynn Ave,
North Vancouver, BC, V7J 2C4, Ph: (604) 980 9852.
NEW ZEALAND: Distributed by Netlink Distribution
Company, Level 4, 23 Hargreaves St, College Hill,
Auckland 1, Ph: (9) 302 7616.
SOUTH AFRICA: Distributed by PSD Promotions (Pty) Ltd,
PO Box 1175, Isando 1600, SA, Ph: (011) 392 6065, and
CNA Limited, Newsstand Division, PO Box 10799,
Johannesburg 2000, SA, Ph: (011) 491 7500.

SimplyLite Cookbook.
Includes index.
ISBN 1 86396 226 3
1. Cookery. 2. Low-fat diet.
(Series: Australian Women's Weekly Home Library).
641.5638

© ACP Publishing Pty Limited 2001
ABN 18 053 273 546
This publication is copyright. No part of it may be
reproduced or transmitted in any form without the
written permission of the publishers.

The publishers would like to thank: Acorn Trading;
Combo Designs; Dinosaur Designs; Domestic Pots;
Empire Homewares; Grace Bros; Mud Australia;
Orson & Blake Collectables; Prima Cosa; Ruby Star
Traders; Shack; Tatti; The Bay Tree Kitchen Shop; Victoria
Spring Designs; Wheel & Barrow Homewares; and Wok,
Wicker and Spice, for props used in photography.

The publishers would also like to thank Queensland
Fruit & Vegetable Growers and Australian Horticultural
Corporation for their recipe contributions.

Cover: Raspberry poppy seed cake, page 192
Photographer: Ashley Mackevicius
Stylist: Sarah O'Brien
Back cover: Sumac-spiced potato wedges, page 178
Photographer: Ashley Mackevicius
Stylist: Wendy Berecry